CUSTOMER SERVICE LETTERS

READY TO GO!

Cheryl McLean

Printed on recyclable paper

**International Customer
Service Association**

NTC Business Books
a division of *NTC Publishing Group* • Lincolnwood, Illinois USA

Library of Congress Cataloging-in-Publication Data

McLean, Cheryl, 1957-
    Customer service letters ready to go!/ Cheryl Mclean.
       p. cm.
    Published in association with the International Customer Service Association.
    ISBN 0-8442-3567-9 (pbk.)
    1. Customer services. 2. Commercial correspondence. I. Title.
HF5415.5.M39 1995
808'.066658–dc20

95–20176
CIP

Published by NTC Business Books, a division of NTC Publishing Group
4255 West Touhy Avenue,
Lincolnwood (Chicago), Illinois 60646-1975 U.S.A.
© 1996 by NTC Publishing Group, All rights reserved.
No part of this book may be reproduced, stored in a retrieval system,
or transmitted in any form or by any means,
electronic, mechanical, photocopying, recording or otherwise,
without the prior permission of NTC Publishing Group.
Manufactured in the United States of America.

5 6 7 8 9 0 ML 9 8 7 6 5 4 3 2 1

CONTENTS

CHAPTER 4: SAMPLE CUSTOMER SERVICE LETTERS

ACKNOWLEDGMENTS

I would like to thank the many wonderful members of the International Customer Service Association who contributed their advice, expertise, and sample letters for this book. Everyone who uses this book will benefit from their years of experience in this demanding field. Many of these individuals and the companies they work for preferred to remain anonymous, so I extend my thanks collectively. Individually, for contributing sample letters, I want to thank the following:

Jeri Stark
Manager, Order Administration
Symantec Corporation
ICSA Executive Board Member
Chair of Market Research

Ralph F. McKinney
Manager, Specialized Services
Education Loan Servicing Center, Inc.

Kathy S. Harter
Education Loan Servicing Center, Inc.
Secretary
ICSA Indiana Chapter

R. Steven Gunn
Circulation Administration Manager
Newspaper Agency Corporation
1995 President
ICSA Utah/Intermountain Chapter

Howard E. Schryer
Director Customer Service
American Olean Tile
Vice President
ICSA Pennsylvania–New York Chapter

Christina Alberghini
Director of Fulfillment
National Geographic Society
Secretary
ICSA Baltimore/Washington Chapter

Paula Seesman
Manager, Customer Service
National Geographic Society

Vivian A. Taylor
Senior Consumer Information Specialist
Coors Brewing Company Consumer
    Information Center
Treasurer
ICSA Colorado Chapter

Mark O. Nelson
Director of Client Services
Texas/Louisiana District
Cellular One
McCaw Cellular Communications, Inc.
ICSA Executive Board Member
Chair of Communications Committee

Mark Nelson deserves special thanks for helping to direct this project and provide ICSA support. His clear understanding of the needs of customer service professionals and his ability to zero in on important issues were essential in guiding the development of this book. Thanks also to Elizabeth Gleason, of the ICSA Headquarters Office, who provided timely and valuable assistance. I appreciate the patience and direction of my editor, Rich Hagle. And finally, my love and thanks to my mother, Pat McLean, who spent hours on the telephone helping to gather sample letters.

Six Steps to Great Customer Service Letters

What is Customer Service?

Customer service isn't always about complaints and bad news. It's a constant state of awareness, at every level of operations, that the customer is at the heart of your business, and that being responsive to—even anticipating—customer needs will keep you ahead of the competition.

The International Customer Service Association defines customer service as:

- The intangible element that separates good companies from truly great ones.
- What brings value to a transaction between buyer and seller.
- The determining factor in repeat business.
- What will determine if you will be in business by the turn of the century.
- Delivering the customer more than he or she wants, ahead of schedule, and under budget.
- Not everything. It's the *ONLY* thing.

Why Customer Service is Essential

The days of the one-store town, the one-choice telephone company, or the lone express delivery service are long gone. Today, consumers—business buyers as well as individual consumers—have many options for virtually everything they spend money on. One of the most powerful motives behind the choices consumers make is how well they're treated. Since the 1980s, research has consistently shown that consumers value service over other criteria, including price. They want to know *they are valued* by the company.

Those consumers—*your* customers—are your *business*, your reason for being. Without them, you'd cease to exist. Many a company has fallen for failing to provide the service that customers have come to expect. Although companies can exist for a time on one-time customers, word soon spreads that those who've tried your products or services aren't willing to return.

IS THE CUSTOMER ALWAYS RIGHT?

Let's put it this way: Even if the customer isn't right, you don't want to be the one who says so. Begin with the assumption that the customer is right and that your role is to settle the question to the customer's ultimate satisfaction. There are times, however, when the customer is clearly wrong, and your job is to bring the customer around to your viewpoint— without implying fault or blame on the customer's part. The International Customer Service Association Creed, reprinted below, helps establish the customer's proper place: at the center of your business.

THE INTERNATIONAL CUSTOMER SERVICE ASSOCIATION CREED

A CUSTOMER is the most important person in our company.

A CUSTOMER deserves our most courteous and attentive treatment.

A CUSTOMER does not interrupt our work but is rather the purpose of our work.

A CUSTOMER comes to us with needs; it is our job to fulfill them.

A CUSTOMER is part of our company, not an outsider.

A CUSTOMER does not depend on us; rather, we depend on our customer.

A CUSTOMER *IS* our business.

Consumers are becoming increasingly savvy about customer service—and demanding better from companies that don't meet their needs. Books like *Consumer Revenge* or *It's Not My Department! How to Get the Service You Want, Exactly the Way You Want It* give consumers explicit instructions on how to write complaint letters that get results.

Here are six steps for writing customer service letters that result in good customer relations for a variety of situations.

THE SIX STEPS

In the following chapters, we'll discuss the contemporary conventions for the shape letters should take and some specific tips for writing effectively. Here, however, what we're talking about is *strategy*. How do you write the letter to achieve your ultimate goals?

STEP ONE: UNDERSTAND YOUR AUDIENCE

The first step in any correspondence is to find out who you're writing to and how that knowledge might affect what you're going to write. Here are some questions to ask yourself as you begin:

- Is this an individual or a representative of a business or corporation?
- What questions or concerns does the reader have?
- How does the reader feel about your company (product, service)?
- How much influence does the customer have on future sales? (Is this a buyer for a major corporation? Will a mistake risk the customer's goodwill— or your position?)
- What is the customer's general mood—angry? dissatisfied? satisfied? questioning? friendly? indifferent?
- What are the reader's expectations? Why will the reader be interested in your letter?
- What does the reader see as an acceptable response or solution?
- What does the reader already know about this situation?
- How will the reader use the information you present?
- What tone and style will be most effective in reaching this customer?
- How do you want the reader to feel after reading your letter?

Your answers will guide you through the rest of the steps in this process. Put yourself in the position of your customer. What kind of letter would you expect to receive? What information would persuade you to take the action you desire from your customer?

STEP TWO: DEFINE YOUR PURPOSE

The desire to satisfy the customer and to communicate how much your company values that customer's patronage is at the heart of most customer service letters. But within this broad context, you must achieve a *specific purpose*, usually a combination of the following:

Respond to the specific needs or concerns of the customer; and

Achieve the general and specific goals of your organization.

Two of the most basic purposes of business communications are to *inform* and to *persuade*. The informative purpose often achieves your first goal—meeting the customer's needs—while the persuasive purpose works on the second—building customer loyalty.

In some measure, all customer service writing involves a touch of persuasion because you want the customer to retain a positive image of your company. Here are some examples of both purposes, and how even informative letters can—and often should—carry a persuasive message.

Informative Purpose	*Persuasive Purpose*
Explain change in delivery date	Request patience; apologize for delay
Provide requested information	Affirm quality of product or service
Explain reasons for request denial	Express appreciation of continued support
Provide status of account balance	Affirm company's service orientation
Make billing adjustment in the customer's favor	Affirm company quality, desire to pass savings on to valued customers
Explain terms of warranty	Affirm that company stands by its products
Let established customers know about new service, product, sales	Assure their value to the company; company's quality or responsiveness
Announce policy changes	Affirm open-door policy

This list illustrates how even a simple letter explaining the terms of a product warranty can become an opportunity to sell your company as one that stands by its products, is committed to serving its customers, and has the customers' interests as its number one priority. But it's by no means an exhaustive list.

STEP THREE: SET THE RIGHT TONE

Once you understand the audience and define your purpose, you have the information you need to determine the tone your letter should take. Yes, the written word has a "tone of voice," which often communicates more loudly than the words themselves. Too often, letters from companies sound so formal and stuffy that the reader doesn't try wading through the verbiage. On the other hand, it's possible to be too flippant or "cute" in a letter to a customer who might see the attitude as ungracious or offensive.

One word defines the overall tone of every good customer service letter: *respectful.*

Whether you want to be firm or friendly, formal or casual, your letter should always be respectful, courteous, and reasonable. Put yourself in the place of the reader who receives the following:

Dear Ms. Wilson:

I received your letter, but I couldn't see what you had to complain about with the service at Dino-Dips. Our servers are kept very busy and have more important things to do than heat baby bottles. You should be responsible for such special individual requirements as we can't possibly anticipate your every need.

Respectfully,

Jane Doe
Customer Service Associate

Closing with "respectfully" does nothing to mitigate the damage done by the disrespectful tone of the letter itself. It communicates that not only is the customer's concern considered stupid, but that the customer herself is thought frivolous and of little value to the letter writer.

This example also lacks another message that your tone should convey: appreciation. Let your customer know that you appreciate hearing of problems and concerns as well as compliments—even when you're writing bad news.

The tone with which you write will depend in large measure on whether you're writing with good news, bad news, or routine information. Here are some guidelines for each.

■ The Good News Letter

A letter bearing only good news is naturally the customer service representative's favorite. The tone can be *positive, informal,* and *friendly* and achieve both informative and persuasive goals fairly easily. Good news letters don't have to wait for the customer to complain but can anticipate problems or extend goodwill gestures to keep your company in the customer's mind. Some examples of good news situations include:

- Expressing thanks for a complimentary letter about the company, or a product, service, or employee.
- Notifying customers of refunds, rebates, gifts, or other specific tangible benefits.
- Announcing changes in policy that benefit customers.
- Thanking customers for their patronage, help with customer survey, fund-raising event attendance, recommending the company to a friend, or a good suggestion.
- Granting customer requests.
- Offering special service to long-time customers.
- Sending a follow-up letter to be sure the customer was satisfied with the replacement product, repair service, or response received about a complaint.

Here are some tips for setting an informal, friendly tone:

- Use *I* and *you*.
- Write as if you were conversing directly with your reader.
- Use contractions such as *you're, it's, I'm, we're, isn't*.
- Use smaller, more familiar words; for example, *letter* insteac of *correspondence, use* instead of *utilize, pay* for *recompense, also* for *furthermore*.

Consider this example:

> I want to thank you for your letter requesting a refund on the tickets you purchased to the Simons Brothers concert December 6 because you were expecting a rock concert rather than gospel music. It's important for me to get feedback from listeners like you so that Dapper Productions can better schedule the concerts you want.
>
> Although I can't refund your money, I've enclosed a voucher for two free tickets to any of this year's Dapper Productions concerts. If you're not sure about the style of music being presented, please call me at (206) 555-1122 and I'll fill you in. Thank you again for your comments, and enjoy your next concert.

The letter addresses the reader as someone with legitimate concerns, then proceeds to deny the request while offering a different compensation. The tone takes into account the audience—a rock concert lover who is dissatisfied—and the purpose—satisfy both the customer's need to be compensated for a disappointing experience and the company's no-refund policy and encourage the customer to return.

■ *The Bad News Letter*

It's easy to write with a positive tone when the news is good. The real challenge is to write a letter that sends bad news but makes the customer come back with a smile. The tone, in this case, might be *firm* but *friendly*, *sympathetic*, and *reasonable*. Some examples of bad news letters include:

- Refusing customer requests.
- Recalling defective merchandise.
- Refusing credit.
- Notifying the customer that the ordered product is no longer available.
- Denying claims or requests for adjustment.
- Explaining that an order doesn't meet the company's minimum order requirements.

In some cases, you might be able to add a *positive* element, offering an alternative or some means of recompense that might alleviate some of the customer's dissatisfaction.

Be wary, though, of using some of the standard closing statements that tell customers you're delighted to serve them or that ask them to call if they need further assistance. If you've just turned down their request, they won't feel well served, and you don't want to leave room for misinterpreting your decision as less than final.

Sometimes you may want to take refuge in more *formal* language that establishes an *impersonal* tone. This tone is not as appropriate when you need to placate a customer, but you can use it effectively to state firm decisions that cannot be appealed with further complaints.

- Use *the company* or *we* rather than *I*.
- Use passive voice rarely but wisely; for example, *the loan request could not be granted* removes an individual from the "bad guy" role because the person denying the request is hidden. Passive voice can also help avoid making accusations. For example, *When the seal on the computer housing was opened by someone other than an authorized repair center, the warranty was nullified* sounds better than *Because you broke the housing seal, you voided the warranty*.
- Use courteous, respectful language that is clear and concise.

■ Don't use big words to sound important (see Chapter 3).

■ Use complete words rather than contractions.

Here's an example:

> Thank you for your recent inquiry about your automotive loan.
>
> We regret that Superior Finance, Ltd., is unable to change the name, address, or social security number assigned to this loan. The person who signed the promissory note is legally responsible for repayment and must remain on our permanent records until the debt is cleared.
>
> Please call our office at (322) 555-2211 if we may be of assistance in some other way.

This letter will most likely generate a return call from the customer. You might want to consider a telephone call instead to simplify the whole transaction.

It's possible, also, to craft your letter with a tone of voice that is both personal and semi-formal, communicating firm professionalism as well as concern for the reader as an individual. The use of language in writing letters that communicate clearly is covered more fully in Chapter 3.

■ *The Routine Reply Letter*

Routine replies—those that send neither good news nor bad—take their tone from your company's general policy on customer service. Such policies vary from an informal, personal approach to a formal, more traditional style.

Most of these letters will be brief and to the point, with little room for setting a tone of either friendliness or formality. All letters, however, can include some suggestion of the company's appreciation of its customers. Here are some examples:

> Thank you for your continued interest in James Brothers.

■ ■ ■

> We appreciate the opportunity to serve you.

■ ■ ■

If I can be of further assistance, please call my direct phone number, 555-2381.

■ ■ ■

Remember, we are always here to help you, 24 hours a day. We look forward to hearing from you soon.

STEP FOUR: DETERMINE THE DESIRED RESPONSE

What do you want the reader to do with the information you present? What is the reaction you hope to achieve? Do you want the reader to do something specific—pick up the phone, stop by for a refund, return the product for a replacement? Or do you simply want to foster a positive attitude?

While this step is related to defining the letter's purpose, there's an important distinction that will affect how you organize your message (Step Six). If you've presented bad news but want to keep the customer relationship strong, you might want to enclose some kind of compensation that has the customer returning (such as a discount coupon toward the next purchase). This can succeed in turning the customer's reaction from disgruntled acceptance of the bad news to being impressed with the company's responsiveness.

When you want a specific action or response from the reader, your message must be persuasive enough to elicit such action. You want to build your argument and end with a strong "call to action" statement.

To help us serve you better, please take a moment to complete the attached information card.

■ ■ ■

I've enclosed a postage-paid return authorization for your convenience. Simply repackage the product, apply the detachable label, and drop it in your mailbox. We'll take care of everything else. You will receive your replacement product by overnight delivery.

■ ■ ■

Please call me to arrange a time, at your convenience, when our repair crew can service your new energy-efficient gas furnace.

Each of these examples asks for a specific action from the customer and promises a timely, helpful response in return. Sometimes, however, the response you want is simply continued goodwill, patience, or understanding. In these instances, the closing paragraph would include a sincere statement affirming the company's esteem for the customer, appreciation for valuable feedback, or willingness to serve.

STEP FIVE: ORGANIZE YOUR MESSAGE

All letters written to customers need to be thoughtfully organized to give the best impression possible and to most effectively communicate your message to your customer. The reader must be able to follow your reasoning, and the letter should move logically from stating the problem and its importance to the suggested solution. The closing should always be positive—whether you're writing with good news or bad.

■ *The Good News Approach*

- Begin with a positive note—congratulations, praise, appreciation.
- Address the reader's primary concern and make clear why it's important.
- State what action, if any, was taken and any qualifications or conditions that apply.
- Reaffirm your company's integrity, quality, concern, or goals that will give the reader the positive impression you want to convey.
- Request the desired reader response.
- Briefly restate the good news in closing, or express your desire for future interaction (sales, service) or your thanks for the customer's continued confidence in your firm.

■ *The Bad News Approach*

- Begin with a "buffer" statement, something neutral that introduces the reader's concern or expresses appreciation. You want to communicate that your reader's concerns are important to you and that you understand the problem.
- Give clear, briefly stated reasons for the bad news first. And whatever you do, don't use "company policy" as an excuse. There must be a reason for that policy in the first place, so explain the specific rationale for your decision.
- If you haven't already, make a clear, tactful statement of the decision or action. Don't imply fault. Don't apologize.

- Offer an alternative solution or compensation, a compromise, or an incentive for doing future business whenever possible.

- Close on a positive, courteous note. Don't restate the problem, invite further questions, or suggest that there might be further problems (*e.g., if you experience any other difficulty, please call*).

■ The Routine Reply

- Begin with a note of thanks and a clear statement of your reason for writing (answer customer inquiry, provide requested information, update order schedule, change delivery date).

- Provide specific information, important details, explanation, or necessary actions.

- Close with thanks, offer of future assistance, or invitation to do further business.

STEP SIX: MAKE IT PERSONAL AND READABLE

What are the two most sure-fire ways to have your reader toss your letter into the round file (a.k.a. trash can) without reading it?

1. Addressing your letter to "Occupant," and

2. Burying your message in so much text that the reader gets tired of wading through it before the second paragraph.

The solution? Personalize your letters and keep them simple.

■ Personal Responses Versus Form Letters

In Step Four, we discussed setting the proper tone for your letter, including personal and impersonal. *Personal*, in this step, means directing your letter to a specific individual—your customer, by name—whenever possible. Form letters save time, but they tell your customers you're too busy to take a personal interest in their concerns. Form letters suggest you've given the request a quick look, just enough to decide which form letter to send. You want to weigh the customer's interpretation of a form letter—and how that may affect the customer's feelings about your company—against the time and money you save in the short run.

This doesn't mean that you have to abandon form letters completely. On the contrary, having ready-made replies not only helps speed your responses but assures you're sending consistent messages and maintaining a consistent level of quality in your customer service.

With the growth and sophistication of computers in the workplace, however, personalizing letters has become as simple as typing the customer's name and address. Word processing and database software programs make it easy to create several "form" letters, with room for the name, address, and salutation to be added just before printing. If your company deals in hundreds of standard replies daily, you're still only entering the names and addresses in the computer—which is faster than writing them by hand onto preprinted forms.

Major corporations with mainframe computers can use special management programs such as Napersoft's Automated Correspondence System. Once you've created your standard letters, the computer prompts customer service personnel to select the appropriate document, enter the customer information, and print the letter and envelope ready for mailing. If the representatives have the authorization, they can add a case-specific sentence or paragraph to further personalize the letter.

But even smaller organizations with personal computers can take advantage of the print merging capabilities found in most word processing programs. Database programs, too, can keep customer names and addresses up-to-date and facilitate personalizing your letters.

Sometimes, especially with routine information letters, you need to take the mass approach because addressing 25,000 letters to specific individuals can't be justified in terms of cost or efficiency. In these instances, it's okay to say *Dear Acme customer* and use the same letter for everyone. When you're responding to an individual complaint or question, however—even if you receive a hundred of the same questions every day—using the personal approach will help your customer relationships stay positive.

Another important point about form letters: If you *are* sending out hundreds of the same letters, you may need to ask if there are some proactive steps you can take to resolve the issue before customers complain. If a lot of customers are having difficulty understanding your shipping instructions, for example, it's probably time to revise your instruction sheet.

■ *Keep It Simple*

Letter writing sometimes does strange things to otherwise down-to-earth, friendly people. It can make us sound stuffy, staid, even pompous and stiff. We think that only by using "big" words can we project the image of the confident, knowledgeable professional. By adding a lot of unnecessary verbiage, we think we're following the correct form for the business epistle established by earlier, loftier generations.

Wrong. The craft of letter writing has, over the years, developed dead wood that deserves to be chopped. Here are a few examples of oversize logs cut down to efficient kindling:

due to the fact that	*because*
at the present time	*now*
in the near future	*soon*
reached a mutual agreement	*agreed*

Chapter 3 expands on the need for simplicity, giving several specific tips for crafting letters that communicate clearly, concisely, and effectively.

POTENTIAL PITFALLS

By following the steps outlined above, and especially by setting the proper respectful tone in your replies to your customers, you'll likely avoid the most obvious pitfall to writing customer service letters—offending the customer. Another pitfall—failing to provide the service desired—is often out of your hands because the customer's request is unreasonable, the company's policies prohibit offering the compensation requested, or the customer sees a problem when there isn't one. But the most potentially expensive of the pitfalls facing a customer service representative is when the customer threatens to sue.

■ LEGAL ISSUES IN CUSTOMER COMPLAINTS

Sometimes the threat of a lawsuit can be implied in the letter without being stated explicitly. When you encounter one of these situations, turn the issue over to your company's legal department or legal representative. Recognizing potential legal issues and seeking legal counsel can help you keep your company from litigation.

There are a variety of laws that hold businesses accountable to their customers. As consumers become more sophisticated in their demands, they are also more aware of these laws. Only your lawyer can help you determine whether the threat is justified. Here are some of the most common issues in business law:

- misrepresentation
- fraud
- liability
- breach of contract

Misrepresentation generally applies to advertisements that the customer claims misrepresent the truth. Truth in Advertising laws require that statements made in advertising be fully supportable. Even if the advertised information was a misprint caused by the newspaper or magazine in which it was printed, unless the company acted quickly to correct the error, the company can be held accountable.

Fraud can involve advertising, misrepresentation by sales or other company personnel, mail order catalogue misrepresentation, or failure of a product to meet the *implied warranty of merchantability*. This means that if a product is defective or does not meet the basic standards of salability, selling it can be considered fraudulent.

Liability is the most serious of legal issues and the one most likely to involve both higher courts and larger settlements. Liability suits claim damages, sometimes both actual damages—costs associated with personal injury, loss of income, or physical property damage—and punitive damages—money awarded by the court to punish the company for having acted irresponsibly or with gross negligence. Liability suits can be based on faulty products, improper workmanship, improper labeling, or any number of other issues.

Breach of contract or agreement involves claims that the company violated an agreement with the customer. The agreement can be in writing, or it can be implied in the act of selling merchandise or services, or it can be a verbal agreement between the customer and a sales representative of the company.

■ LEGAL ISSUES IN CUSTOMER SERVICE LETTERS

Any time you commit yourself to paper, you need to be careful of your language not only for the sake of communicating clearly but because you don't want to give your customer grounds for legal action against your company. The categories of legal action listed above provide some clues about how you can avoid adding fuel to the potential fire.

How do you think a legal eagle would look at the following lines in a letter from a company to a customer?

> We're very sorry that our slippery floors caused you to fall and break your hip.

■ ■ ■

Your mail-order catalogue did not get posted by the date specified in our contract because the sorted bags were mismarked and misplaced in the mailroom. We apologize for any inconvenience.

■ ■ ■

The advertisement you refer to was mistaken. The free wheel alignment offered with tire sales is given only with the purchase of a fifth tire.

■ ■ ■

The sales associate you spoke with misrepresented our company policy; we regret we cannot honor your request.

In each instance, the letter admits to a potentially litigious responsibility. In the first, the letter admits that the floors were slippery and that the slippery floors caused the customer's broken hip. Get ready to pay for hospital bills, emotional duress, lost income, and attorney's fees. The second admits to negligence in a situation that could cost your company for the mail order catalogue company's loss of revenue as well as breach of contract. The third item admits that the advertisement presented false or misleading information, and the last states rather baldly that the company's official representative—the sales associate—lied to the customer.

The message here is to be aware of the legal issues and the potential dangers inherent in admitting—on paper—to any specific responsibility. It's just like those old detective movies: What you write can and will be used against you in a court of law.

CONTEMPORARY CONVENTIONS

We're living in the Information Age, the Electronic Age, the Global Village—all catchwords to describe the rapid, sweeping changes that continue to affect the way we communicate. Gone are the days of long letters handwritten in a fine copperplate script. Gone, too, are the more flowery conventions of letter-writing—salutations such as *To a most valued and esteemed gentleman* or closings such as *Your humble servant*. Good riddance.

The age of computers and sophisticated technology has brought more immediate, direct communications links between companies and their customers. A letter can usually cross the country in a matter of days rather than weeks or months. With facsimile transmissions and computer modems linked to the Internet, communication happens in an instant.

While the new media require some additional rules of etiquette, some time-honored conventions of letter-writing still apply. Here's a checklist to use for writing letters in today's business world.

CHECKLIST: BASIC PARTS OF A CUSTOMER SERVICE LETTER

A well-designed letterhead speaks volumes about your company image, and a well-formatted letter tells your customers that you are treating their concern with professional care and attention. The letterhead should include the company name and address, so there's no need to repeat this information in the body of your letter.

Always include the date of your correspondence at least two line spaces under the letterhead, either flush with the left margin or flush left to the center of the page. The customer's name and address should begin two lines below the date, always flush with the left margin. Start the salutation two lines below the address, also flush left, and followed by a colon. Two lines below that, begin the letter, either with or without an indent.

In the body of the letter, leave a single line space between paragraphs. Your closing should be separated from the body of the text by a single line space and placed in the same position as the date, either flush left or center. Leave enough room for your signature, usually three to four lines, then include your full name and title on two lines aligned with the closing.

The following letters demonstrate three standard styles, all of which are acceptable in business correspondence.

■ *Block Style*

December 3, 1995

Ms. Delia Adams
222 First Street
Anytown, CO 30503

Dear Ms. Adams:

The block style letter keeps all information flush to the left margin. Notice that the state name in the address line uses the two-letter postal abbreviation in capital letters.

This simplifies computer database management so that the address can be entered once for both the letter and the envelope. If you prefer, however, the state name can be spelled out on the letter.

After the writer's name and title lines, type the initials of the letter writer in capital letters, followed by a colon or virgule (/) and the typist's initials in lower case. Often customer service officials type their own letters, so this line is unnecessary.

Leave two or three line spaces between the closing and your typed name for your signature.

Sincerely,

Cheryl McLean
Customer Service Manager

CM:mr

■ *Modified Block Style*

December 5, 1995

Mr. Steven Miller
332 Southwest Fifth Street
Mainville, OR 97322

Dear Mr. Miller:

The modified block style provides a little visual relief, with the date and closing set off-center and body paragraphs indented approximately five letter spaces. This is considered somewhat old-fashioned but is still a popular style.

This letter demonstrates other standard additions at the bottom of a letter. The word "Enclosure," sometimes abbreviated "Enc.," announces that something is enclosed with the letter. If there is more than one enclosure, sometimes the individual items are listed, as below.

When you are sending copies of this letter to others, indicate who will be receiving copies after the initials "cc" and a colon. Although it actually stands for "carbon copy," something that has gone the way of the dinosaurs, "cc" is still the standard indication that other copies are being sent, whether they're photocopies or electronic.

Use "bc" if you are sending a "blind copy"—one where the primary recipient's name is masked when sent to others. The names are arranged alphabetically for simplicity, but can be arranged by title or position on the company's organizational chart.

Sincerely yours,

Cheryl McLean
Customer Service Manager

Enclosures: Invoice
            Copy of transaction letter

cc: J. Ahlers, Acme President
    C. Renwick, Acme Accounting Manager
    D. Steens, Acme Sales Manager

■ *Simplified Style*

November 12, 1995

Chris Waite
P.O. Box 2233
Citytown, CA 90210

SUBJECT: CHANGE IN ACCOUNT STATUS

The question of the customer's gender, discussed under "Salutation" in the text below, becomes moot with this letter style because the salutation is omitted in exchange for a subject line. This form is adequate for transmitting routine information but would be less appropriate for sending a "bad news" letter, where your intent is to lead gently into the subject rather than announce it baldly in capital letters.

In this case, the closing line, too, can be omitted. The letter can be signed or not, whichever you prefer. The writer's name and title are typed in capital letters, and if someone other than the author has typed the letter, only the typist's initials appear below. This form is also appropriate for facsimile transmissions.

CHERYL MCLEAN
CUSTOMER SERVICES MANAGER

dd
Enc.

SALUTATION: A CONTEMPORARY APPROACH

While the formatting of a letter is simple, figuring out how to address your audience can be a little tricky. The standard salutation word is still "Dear," and unless you're on a first-name basis with your customer, you would use the courtesy title with the last name. But which courtesy title to use?

With men, that's easy: *Mr.* But changing social conventions have made addressing women customers a sometimes knotty issue. The contemporary approach is to use *Ms.*, coined so that women were not addressed according to their marital status. However, when your customer signs herself "Mrs. John Smith," respect her preference and use "Mrs. Smith" in your reply.

But what if the customer's name is Dana, Terry, Jan, or Chris? Or perhaps the letter was signed "A.R. Johnson." The simplest solution is to use the full name in the salutation: "Dear A.R. Johnson" or "Dear Terry White." Or use the simplified block style that omits the salutation line. Avoid using generic terms such as "Dear Acme Customer" because this tells the reader that this is a form letter—unless, of course, it *is* a form letter.

COMMUNICATIONS MEDIA: MAKING THE RIGHT CHOICE

The Information Age has brought about a range of options for communicating with your customers, and it's sometimes difficult to know which medium to choose for sending your message. All of the options have advantages and disadvantages.

If you're responding to a customer, take your cue from the customer. You want to choose the same medium, unless the customer specifically requests otherwise, because, as communications specialist and futurist Marshall McLuhan once wrote, the "medium is the message." The medium your customer chooses sends you an unwritten message about what your customer wants from you.

TELEPHONE

The customer who uses the telephone wants immediate attention, communicating one-on-one with a person who can be responsive. Sometimes the customer is upset or angry or frustrated and looking for someone to bear the brunt of these emotions. In this case, you can sometimes diffuse the emotions by requesting time to look into the matter thoroughly before you call back. By the time you return the call, the customer's had a chance to cool off, and you've been able to plan your strategy.

The down side of using the telephone is that if you revisit an issue, you must depend on your memory of the conversation, unless you've kept written notes on file. A written communication provides a traceable "paper trail" of the company's interactions with the customer that can be helpful in many situations.

The telephone is not generally used in customer relations to provide unsolicited information, both because the cost is prohibitive and because many customers see unsolicited telephone calls as an intrusion.

LETTERS

When a customer writes a letter, several messages come through. The customer may not feel comfortable in a one-on-one conversation, preferring a slower but less confrontational approach. The time taken to sit down and write the letter suggests the customer is serious or perhaps wants documentation.

In most cases, the proper response to a customer's letter is another letter. Some exceptions to this general rule might be when the timing requires a more immediate response, when you need more information before you can fully respond, or when the response or solution is too complex for a letter and could be better explained directly. For example, a customer who complains that a computer from your company freezes up when running a word processing program, your technical support staff member can walk the customer through the steps to resolve the problem over the telephone rather than risk misunderstanding by explaining them in writing.

FACSIMILE (FAX)

Most of your corporate customers, and many individuals, have the capability of sending and receiving written correspondence instantly over the telephone lines. The customer who faxes a letter is most likely asking for a rapid response.

With the increasing postage costs, sometimes it's simply cheaper as well as faster to send a letter by fax. The sender pays nothing for local calls and can pay as little as 12 to 20 cents to send a long-distance fax. That looks pretty good against the cost of a first-class stamp and three- to five-day delivery.

Some letter form conventions change to accommodate the new medium. Many companies have revised their standard letter form to avoid the need for a separate facsimile cover page, which reduces the sender's phone costs and the uses less paper on the receiver's end.

The simplest way to indicate that the letter is being sent electronically is to add, at the top of the page, the words *VIA FACSIMILE*, underlined or highlighted for emphasis, then the sending and receiving fax numbers and the number of pages being sent. The rest of the letter appears as it would in a standard format. A post script can be added with the number to call if the facsimile did not transmit completely.

Some companies create specific letterhead for use with faxed letters that clearly present the company name, address, and phone and fax numbers, as well as an "Attention" line for naming the intended recipient and spaces for indicating the number of pages and the receiving fax number. In this case, the address line is simply the recipient's fax number.

Here's an example of how to put together a standard fax cover sheet or letter form:

FAST-LANE SUPPLIES, INC.

233 Market Street • P.O. Box C124 • Portland, OR 97222
Voice (503) 555-2211 • Fax (503) 555-1221

FAST-LANE FAX

[1] pages (including this page)

January 23, 1996

TO: Jane Smythe, Purchasing Director
212/555-2553

FROM: Arnold Pearson, Industrial Relations

— —

Dear Jane:

Thank you for bringing the problem with delayed deliveries to my attention. I've spoken with the chief of shipping operations and the trucking representative. I'm happy to assure you that future shipments will arrive as scheduled via an alternative freight company.

To help compensate for the previous inconvenience, Fast-Lane will pick up the shipping tab on your next order. I look forward to talking with you.

Please call (503) 555-2211 if this facsimile was not received in full.

ELECTRONIC MAIL

More than 30 million people worldwide are connected to the Internet, the international network of computers that links corporations with governments, libraries, universities, and individuals via computer modems and telephone lines. This vast communications network is growing rapidly to include even more individuals and organizations. One of the primary reasons people choose to go "on line" is to gain access to electronic mail, or *e-mail*.

E-mail allows users to send messages instantly from one computer to another, either across town or across continents. Formatted like memos, e-mail letters are sent to the individual's e-mail "address," a string of unbroken letters or numbers that looks like a string of typos. In reality, the address stands for the individual's on-line "name," the location of the main server computer to which he or she subscribes, and whether that computer belongs to an organization, an educational institution, a governmental agency, a military organization, a network, or a private company.

More and more companies are publicizing their e-mail addresses to facilitate communications with customers. The Hayes modem corporation, for example, has customers send warranties in electronically and has a special e-mail address for technical questions.

E-mail is used especially in business-to-business communications. Many of your business clients may be on line and prefer to quickly send electronic messages rather than waste paper, postage (e-mail communications are generally free), and time sending what's known in the cyber world as "snail mail."

SPECIAL CONVENTIONS FOR E-MAIL

The ease and speed of electronic mail have affected the traditional letter form as it applies to this new medium of communication. People who use e-mail frequently, especially those in large corporations in which all employees are connected, can be inundated with messages. The same message can be sent to hundreds of people with a few simple commands, which also increases the volume of mail. The result is that e-mail messages are generally kept short and direct, formatted like a memorandum, with the "to" and "from" lines being the full e-mail addresses.

ELECTRONIC MAIL ADDRESSES

E-mail addresses seem like so much gibberish, but once you break down the individual parts, they start to make sense. The addresses are determined by the network server—the main computer through which you gain access to electronic mail. Most individuals gain access through commercial information services such as America Online, Compuserve, Prodigy, or Delphi. Major corporations, universities, government agencies, and large organizations may have their own network servers.

The address is divided into sections, separated by periods but no spaces. Each section can be no longer than eight characters. The first section is the user's identification name, or *userid.* Each network server assigns userids differently. The state of Oregon government uses the employee's first name, a period, and the last name. Compuserve names are usually a series of numbers. At America Online, users select their own names or nicknames.

With traditional addresses, what follows the name is the street address. In the case of Internet addresses, the street-level address is the name of the computer server. An "at" sign, @, separates the userid from the server name. If the server is at an institution that has more than one server, the institution name might follow the server name, separated by a period.

Within the United States, addresses generally end with the three-letter indicator of the Internet "domain" within which the server resides. Internationally, and in some instances within the U.S., a two-letter country code is appended to the domain, following a period. The six "domains" are as follows:

- commercial *(com)*
- educational *(edu)*
- organization, usually nonprofit *(org)*
- military *(mil)*
- network *(net)*
- government *(gov)*—or *(st)* for state government

Putting it all together, here's what an Internet address looks like:

cherylmacb@aol.com

What this address means is that cherylmacb "resides" at America Online in the commercial domain of the Internet. Notice that all letters are lower case. That's because the Internet mail network isn't case-sensitive, so whether you type in all capitals or all lower case, the address will read the same. Lower case has become the standard. Here's another example:

jane.doe@or.st.us

In this case, Jane Doe resides at the state of Oregon's server in the United States.

Electronic mail addresses are becoming increasingly visible on business cards and company letterheads, in the signature lines of letters, and in publications and advertisements. Organizations, corporations, and government agencies are recognizing that electronic mail makes it easy for customers—whether business customers or individuals—to communicate.

ETIQUETTE ON THE INTERNET

This new medium has developed its own etiquette, and it's important to understand some of these unwritten rules to avoid unintentionally offending someone. The language of the Internet tends toward spoken rather than written communication, which often lends an informality to messages that isn't as appropriate in traditional letters. A common salutation, for example, is "Hello" or the even more colloquial "Hi." People are almost always on a first-name—or even nickname—basis on the Internet.For the customer service professional, however, a balance between formal and cas ual might serve best.

Here are some other conventions for on-line messages:

- Because e-mail is like a memorandum, the salutation and closing or signature lines are not necessary, but can be used to create a more personal communication.

- Use short one- or two-sentence paragraphs, separated by an extra line space. This makes the messages easier to read on the computer screen.

- Don't shout. How does one shout electronically? BY TYPING IN ALL CAPITAL LETTERS!!! AND USING TOO MANY EXCLAMATION POINTS!!!

- Put an *asterisk* before and after the word that you would ordinarily underline or italicize for emphasis. Internet communications, thus far, are strictly ASCII text, which means that accents or type variations such as bold or italic type do not transfer.

- Acknowledge any e-mail message, whether with your timely reply or with a quick note saying the message was received with thanks or that action will be taken and a more specific reply will follow. Most e-mail software incorporates a "reply" feature— simply click on a reply button and a new message is automatically addressed to the individual who sent the original message.

VISUAL LANGUAGE: A WINK AND A SMILE

Although not something you will be likely to use in your customer service communications, it's good to be aware of *emoticons* or *smileys*. These are a kind of visual language, little tricks of type that form icons to communicate emotions or expressions.

Because electronic mail is like speaking but without the body language or voice intonations that help communicate the speaker's attitude, smileys help set the mood or interpret the intentions of the speaker. They're intended to be viewed with your head tipped to the left . Here are some of the most common examples:

:-) *a smile*   :-o *surprise*

;-) *a wink and a smile*   :-/ *chagrin*

:-(*a sad face*

Whole books have been devoted to listing the various smileys and their meanings. Where they might be useful to the customer service professional is in communicating with business clients who are well-versed in the electronic world. When you have to admit to having missed a deadline, ending the sentence with the chagrined smiley can elicit a smile from your customer.

Advantages and Disadvantages to E-mail Communications

The advantages are pretty clear: no transmission cost, once you're connected to an online server; instant communications; reduced paper clutter; and a simplicity of form. E-mail is also remarkably quick and easy to use.

But there are several disadvantages. One is the fact that you cannot assume privacy in communications. Someone with the know-how can access and read your messages or intercept them as they travel the information superhighway to their destination. This is not generally a problem, but you might be in an industry that requires an extra level of security that may or may not exist on the Internet.

Another disadvantage is the flip side of its major advantage: its speed and ease of use. When people are angry or upset, it's easy to fire off a memo. When someone sends an angry message in the electronic world, it's called *flaming*.

As a customer service representative, you're likely to be on the receiving end of these reactionary messages. It's important to keep your cool and respond with your usual professionalism—no matter how tempting it may be to hit the "reply" button immediately and respond in kind.

Electronic communications are only going to continue to grow in popularity and universality. If your company is not already on line, you might want to investigate the options for giving your customers this new means of communicating with you. You might be surprised at how many of your customers are already connected. The "wave of the future" is here.

3

Tips for
Better Writing

Contrary to popular belief, you don't need to be the next Ernest Hemingway or Virginia Woolf to be good at writing. Your letter writing can sizzle with quality if you follow some basic guidelines.

USE ACTION WORDS

The goal of most writing is to communicate with readers without numbing their brains. You don't want your letters to be kept by the bedside as an effective soporific. Often you want your readers to respond in a positive way or to take some specific action.

Action is the operative word. If you want action, you have to fill your prose with active language. The active part of every sentence is the verb, the spark that energizes the sentence. The problem with a lot of business writing is that many professionals believe if they write as they speak they won't sound like the professionals they are. Look at this sentence:

> The director made a choice to have a meeting with sales representatives so that a discussion could be held regarding how customers have had a negative response to the advertising campaign.

What are the verbs? *Made, have, could be, have had.* The most active of these is *made*, but its action is spurious. The director didn't *make* anything. The director *chose*. Using action verbs requires you to put the action into the verb itself. Ask what the director *did*? What *action* does the sentence describe? Ask these questions of the rest of the sentence. Here's what you get if you activate the verbs:

> The director chose to meet with sales representatives to discuss how customers have responded negatively to the advertising campaign.

This sentence is still cluttered, but we'll cover that in the next section. To activate verbs, find the core of the action, then use the verb for that action. Here are some classic examples of active, sentence-driving verbs being stalled by helper verbs, such as *make, have,* or *be,* or vague, general verbs such as *provide, perform,* or *put.*

STALLED	ACTIVE
make a statement about	state, say
make a decision/choice/payment	decide/choose/pay
make an acquisition of	buy, acquire
make a suggestion/comparison	suggest/compare
make the recommendation/assumption	recommend/assume
give consideration to	consider
have a discussion/belief about	discuss/believe
have the capability	can
have a preference for/intention of	prefer/intend
seems to be suggestive of	suggests
reach an agreement/conclusion	agree/conclude
put into implementation	implement, start
put in place	place, start
provide documentation of	document
provide information for	inform
provide support for	support
make a resolution	resolve
perform a review of	review
perform a service to	serve

This list is by no means exhaustive, but you get the idea. Rev the engines. Get your verbs into the driver's seat of your sentences. That's the first step to writing with clear and concise language.

USE ACTIVE VOICE (BUT KNOW WHEN PASSIVE VOICE SERVES ITS PURPOSE)

The active voice, like active verbs, brings life and energy to your sentences. *Voice* refers to the verb form. With *passive* voice, the person or thing performing the verb's action—the actor—is placed after the verb, becoming the object rather than the subject. Sometimes the actor is missing altogether. Consider the following sentences:

The company's policies have been revised by the vice president.

The company's policies have been revised.

The vice president revised company policies.

The first two sentences are examples of passive voice. What is the verb—the action—of the sentence? *Revised.* Who is the actor? The second example gives no clue, which is the problem with the passive voice. The active voice, in the third example, puts the actor where it belongs—driving the action of the verb.

Writing in the active voice makes clear who is doing what. It's also a more economic style of writing than the passive voice. A related writing problem—*dead construction*—also contributes to lack of clarity and wordiness. Consider these two sentences, the first passive dead construction and the second a trim active construction:

There are seven telephones that the Communications Systems Manager needs to have replaced.

The Communications Systems Manager needs to replace seven telephones.

The words *there are, there is,* and *it is* are your clues to dead construction. Usually, as with passive voice or stalled verbs, all you need to do is find the spark of action, then use the right verb to describe that action. Here are some more examples, with the spark of action—the true verb—italicized, then reused:

It is with *regret* that this letter is written to inform you of the change in your loan status.

I *regret* to inform you of your changed loan status.

■ ■ ■

There are many opportunities *offered* at Acme Finance for customers to expand their portfolio holdings.

Acme Finance *offers* many opportunities for customers to expand their portfolio holdings.

■ ■ ■

Proof of purchase must be *provided* before a refund can be *sent* by the cashier's office.

Please *provide* proof of purchase so the cashier can *send* your refund.

Here are some questions to ask yourself when you're not sure whether you've written with active verbs in the active voice:

■ Does *there are, it is,* or *there is* kill the action of the verb?

■ What is the *action* of the sentence?

■ Who is the *actor?*

■ Is the *actor* performing the *action* of the verb?

If the last answer is no, then find the spark of action and use it to build a sentence in which the actor drives the engine of the verb.

In some instances, especially with customer service letters that are presenting bad news, passive voice can be a valuable tool. For example, a customer is frustrated with a defective cordless telephone. You've discovered that the customer failed to follow the instructions that require the battery to be charged for 24 hours before being used. Here's where passive voice lets you explain the problem without pointing the finger of blame at your customer.

When the telephone is used before it has been fully charged, it won't store phone numbers in its memory. To correct the problem, leave the telephone plugged in for 24 hours without using it, then reassign the numbers in the memory log.

BE CLEAR AND CONCISE: CUT THE CLUTTER

As writing guru William Zinsser wrote in his classic *On Writing Well:*

Clutter is the disease of American writing. We are a society strangling in unnecessary words, circular constructions, pompous frills, and meaningless jargon.

Zinsser's statement gives us the keys to writing with clarity and conciseness. As he suggests, clutter takes many forms—unnecessary words, circular constructions, pompous frills, meaningless jargon. Without clarity, your meaning is lost. Without conciseness, your reader is lost. Either way, you lose, and so do your customers. Here are some key points to winning letter writing.

CUT THE STRANGLEHOLD OF UNNECESSARY WORDS

The sentence we activated with stronger verbs still suffered a surfeit of unnecessary words. Here's the original version, with a little extra clutter added just for fun:

> The director made a choice to have a meeting with sales representatives at this point in time so that a discussion could be held regarding how customers have had a negative response to the advertising campaign.

When we activate the verbs, we cut through a lot of clutter, but not all:

> The director chose to meet with sales representatives at this point in time to discuss how customers have responded negatively to the advertising campaign.

How many more unnecessary words can be cut? Look at this:

> The director met with sales representatives today to discuss negative customer response to the advertising campaign.

From 36 words in the original to 16. By cutting the clutter, we make the sentence clear and concise—in short, we make it more readable. But stalled verbs aren't the only cause of clutter. Here are some other strangling phrases seen far too often in business correspondence:

STRANGLED	CLEAR AND CONCISE
at a rapid rate	rapidly
aware of the fact that	know
due to the fact that/owing to the fact that	because
on account of	because
the reason is because	because
in spite of the fact that	despite, although
call attention to the fact that	notify, remind
conduct an investigation/test	investigate/test
engage in the alteration of	alter

STRANGLED	CLEAR AND CONCISE
in close proximity to	near
as of now/at the present time	now
at this point in time	now, today
in the near future/recent past	soon/recently
prior to/subsequent to	before/after
during the course of/during the time that	during/while
until such time as	until
with the possible exception of	except
in regard/regard to	about
on condition that	provided
in the majority of situations	usually
at a high level of effectiveness	highly effective
for the purpose of/in order to	to
on the part of	by
in the area of	in
in the event that	if
the question as to whether	whether
there is no doubt but that	doubtless, no doubt
in a transparent manner	clearly, transparently

The strangled phrases above make writing sound heavy, stilted, and dull—*not professional.* When writing to your customers, use an economy of words and you'll achieve better communication. *Make every word count.*

WRITE DIRECT SENTENCES WITH CONCRETE WORDS

Part of making your words count—and being clear in the process—is to write positive, direct statements rather than circular, back-door expressions that leave meaning unclear. For example:

> The change in store policy was not precisely responsible for the mistaken impression that some developed regarding the overall lack of

effectiveness of the sales initiative due to the lowering of some sales figures and despite the fact that there was significant increase in others.

What does it mean? Was the initiative—whatever that was—a failure? Or did "some" only perceive that it failed? The policy change wasn't "precisely" responsible, but what precisely was it? Who are the "some"? What is meant by "lack of effectiveness"? What "figures" lowered or increased? There are so many questions, it's difficult to guess at the meaning to adequately rephrase it so that it makes sense.

Compare the above example with this paragraph:

Although actual sales revenue dropped slightly during the national midwinter clearance sale, sales volume increased. Changing policy to allow larger in-store discounts accounted for the net dollar loss despite increased volume.

The second example presents a clear, concise picture of the relationship between store policy and sales. You know what sales "figures" were up or down, what "initiative" and policy were involved, and how each affected the another.

Making your words count requires choosing the best word to say what you mean. The above examples show how vague, imprecise language—*initiative, figures, effectiveness, impression, some, others*—obscures meaning. Precise word choice results in clear communication.

If one of the Public Broadcasting System's stations asked its customers to *participate in the company's annual renewal initiative,* do you think they'd understand that PBS wants them to renew their membership? Here are some other examples of muddy versus clear language.

Muddy and Vague	*Clear and Concrete*
unfavorable communication	complaint
appropriate procedures	*(list them)*
liquidate assets	sell *(specific items)*
organizational substructures	departments
large structure	seven-story building
suitable time period	three-weeks

As this list suggests, too often we use words that lack precise meanings. To write in a direct, concrete style, remember these maxims:

- Use specific words that carry clear meanings.
- Simplify your language: don't use three words or three syllables when one will do.
- Add concrete examples when using abstract, vague terms.

KILL THE POMPOUS FRILLS, CUT THE JARGON

Passive voice, stalled verbs, unnecessary and muddy words all contribute to the affliction common in business writing known as *pompous bombasticitis*, closely related to *bureaucratosis of the text*. Both maladies have a remedy: deep-cutting surgery. Remove the pomposity, excise the jargon.

Language is pompous when it is self-important or excessively ornate. Webster's Dictionary defines *jargon* variously as:

> confused unintelligible language;
>
> a strange, outlandish, or barbarous language or dialect;
>
> obscure and often pretentious language marked by circumlocutions and long words; and
>
> the technical terminology or characteristic idiom of a special activity or group.

A federal judge in New York called the language in Medicare benefit forms "bureaucratic gobbledygook... a form of officialese, federalese and insurancese and doublespeak." There's also businessese, computerese, engineerese, and so on—the rarefied languages of various professions. The only time jargon is appropriate is when you're writing to members of a specific group, all of whom understand the shorthand terminology of their own sphere. Here are some examples of pomposity that needs surgical removal:

POMPOUS	APPROPRIATE
aforementioned correspondences	these letters
subsequent to rendering a decision	after deciding
numerous	many
facilitate	ease
nominally referred to as	called
sufficient	enough
overview	survey

quantify	measure
optimize	perfect
implement	start, do
at this juncture	now
meaningful dialogue	good discussion
oration	speech
attempt	try

You can find hundreds of other examples, all designed to make the letter-writer sound intelligent and professional and all unnecessarily pretentious. Show no mercy: just kill them.

The list below presents samples of jargon and doublespeak that should be subjected to immediate transplant surgery:

JARGON	CLEAR
formulate a paradigm	design a model
vehicular repository	garage
prioritize	rank
disincentive	deterrent
input	opinion
impact (as a verb)	affect, change, alter
expensewise	in terms of expense
schedulewise	in terms of scheduling
interface	coordinate, cooperate
inoperative	failed, not working
function within stated parameters	work within limits
aggregate	total

CUT THE CLICHÉS AND EMPTY EXPRESSIONS

Many of the phrases that we tack onto letters have become so cliché that they have lost their impact. Like other examples of clutter, these phrases take up a lot of space and say very little.

Cliché	*Better*
in the normal course of events	usually
pursuant to your request	at your request
allow me to make a suggestion	I suggest
please find enclosed herewith	enclosed is
come in contact with	meet
thanking you in advance	thank you
in-depth study	analysis
under separate cover	by parcel post, by air express
please don't hesitate to call me	please call me
for all intents and purposes	*(just drop it)*
needless to say	*(just say it)*
in closing I would like to say	*(just say it)*

Use Correct Grammar, Punctuation and Spelling

When you write a letter on company stationery, you are an official representative. Your letter creates an impression not of you, but of your company. A letter that uses misspelled words, bad grammar, or improper punctuation conveys a sense of carelessness at best, lack of professionalism and laziness at worst.

Keep a dictionary handy, or use the spell-checking function of your word processor. Learn the rules of grammar and punctuation. The guidelines below will serve as good reminders, but they don't cover all the potential problems.

Agreement

One of the most common problems is getting subjects and verbs, pronouns and antecedents, and items in a series to agree with each other. The rules are deceptively simple, but applying them in your writing can be a challenge.

■ *Subject–Verb Agreement*

When you have a plural subject, you need a plural noun. Likewise, a singular subject requires a singular noun. A subject—the person, place, or thing that is creating the action of the verb or being acted upon—is usually plural when there's an *s* added to the end of the word. One word, five words. One business, many businesses.

How do you decide whether the verb is singular or plural? A simple test is to use the verb with *he* and *we*. For example, *he says, we say; she does, we do; it falls, we fall.*

Some subjects are always singular. Here's a list of words that you can count on taking the singular verb form:

anyone	everyone	nothing
anything	it	one
each	much	the number of
either	neither	someone
every	no one	that
everybody	nobody	

Some subjects are always plural. These words always take a plural verb:

both	a number of	they
few	several	those
many	these	

So much for the simple ones. The challenge comes with subjects that can be singular or plural or that sound plural but are really singular. Here are some general guidelines:

■ A subject that stands for a definite unit of measurement, time, or money is singular.

Five miles *is* a long way to run.

■ Don't get confused by words that come between the subject and its verb. Focus on what is responsible for the action of the verb—the true subject—then ignore the rest.

The box of books and letters is on the shelf. *("Box" is the subject, not "books and letters.")*

Everyone, including the general managers of the various departments, is invited to the luncheon. *("Everyone" is still the subject.)*

The stereo, including the speakers, *is* covered by our extended warranty. *("Stereo" is the subject.)*

■ Use plural verbs when parts of the subject are joined by the word *and,* as long as the words combined to make the subject don't refer to the same person, thing or unit.

Two September shipments and one December delivery *were* billed in January.

The general manager and board president *is* Jane Fremont. *(Both refer to the same person.)*

■ Use singular verbs when singular subjects are joined by *or.*

Dana Simon or Ron Fleming is responsible for replying to technical questions.

■ Use a singular verb when the subject is a collective noun—a word that stands for a group of people or things—such as *union, politics, group, committee, management, staff,* or *clientele.*

The group of sales clerks in the shoe department has received a cus-tomer service award. *("Group" is the subject; to avoid confusion, write "The shoe department sales clerks have received....")*

Management has announced a change in policy.

■ When a two-part subject is joined by *or, either...or,* or *neither...nor,* then the verb takes the number of the subject closest to the verb.

Either the documents or the *warranty is* in error.

Neither the modem nor the *telephones have* to be replaced.

■ The subject controls the action of the verb, regardless of where in the sentence the subject appears—before or after the verb.

Accepted into the organization were several new employees. *("Employ-ees" is the subject of "accepted.")*

■ Pronouns take singular verbs if they refer to a unit or general quantity, but plural verbs if they stand for amounts or people.

Most of the merchandise *was* damaged.

Most of the employees *were* present.

■ *Pronoun Agreement*

A pronoun stands in for a noun—person, place, or thing—and must agree in number, gender, and person with the noun it represents. The words listed above as taking singular or plural verbs also always take singular or plural pronouns. Another difficulty is deciding the appropriate gender or person. Here are some examples:

> **wrong number:** Everyone has personal expectations for their work load. *(Everyone is singular but pronoun is plural.)*

> **right:** All of us have personal expectations for our work load. *or* Everyone has personal expectations for his or her work load. *or* All employees have personal expectations for their work load.

■ ■ ■

> **wrong person:** Nike Corporation has their own gym.

> **right:** Nike Corporation has its own gym. *(The organization is not a person.)*

■ ■ ■

> **wrong gender:** Each employee is responsible for his customers. *(This is only appropriate if all employees are male.)*

> **right:** All employees are responsible for their customers. *or* Each employee is responsible for his or her customers.

■ *Gender Agreement*

The last item points to a somewhat controversial issue. In today's business world, however, it's important that language not create an impression that your company is sexist.

Your customers might be offended by your use of the generic *he*—writing as if all managers, doctors, scientists, engineers, bankers, corporate presidents, and so forth, are male even though the term is used generally. Similarly, the generic *she* labels all nurses, secretaries, and cooks as female. It's simple to write around the problem by using the plural form. For example:

Instead of *A customer needs to feel he is valued,* **write** *Customers need to feel valued.*

Also, use words that don't imply a specific gender when you can.

mail carrier for mailman   *salesperson* for salesman

police officer for policeman   *drafter* for draftsman

firefighter for fireman   *representative* for spokesman

personnel or *employees* for manpower   *worker* for crewman

■ *Parallel Structure*

Items in a series or list need to agree in terms of their grammatical structure. Look at the following sentence:

Acme Corporation customers appreciate our friendly sales staff, long-term warranties, and how we have experts to solve problems.

The first two are nouns (*staff, warranties*), but the third is a clause. Here's how to fix it:

Acme Corporation customers appreciate our friendly sales staff, long-term warranties, and problem-solving experts.

Here's an example of a list that lacks parallel structure.

Acme's responsibilities to its customers include:
■ Serving you quickly and respectfully
■ Responding to your questions accurately
■ To assist you with technical support

The last item should read *Assisting you with technical support* to maintain the same grammatical form in each item.

PUNCTUATION

So many of us use punctuation intuitively, not sure but throwing in a few extra commas just in case. Punctuation is a tool to add clarity to your writing. Learning the purpose for each tool helps you become more confident as a business writer.

■ *Periods*

Periods end the sentence. Use them frequently. But make sure you have a complete sentence before you do. Otherwise, you end up with a sentence. That is incomplete. Like the last two and this one. A sentence contains a subject and a verb and completes a thought.

Question marks and exclamation points also end sentences. Use the first only for questions, and use the second rarely because the emphasis it suggests can easily be misinterpreted. If you read *What an idea!* written in response to a suggestion you had proffered, would you be sure that the writer was expressing enthusiasm or sarcasm?

■ *Semicolons*

Semicolons join two complete thoughts (clauses) that are too closely related to be separated into two sentences. Semicolons are not used with conjunctions such as *and* or *but;* however, they are used with words like *however, therefore, consequently,* and *instead* when these words introduce the second clause.

Semicolons also separate items in a series when one or more of the items includes commas. For example:

> The following stores offer licensed repairs: Sonny's Radio, Atlanta, GA; G & J Audio, Seattle, WA; and Market Sound, Fresno, CA.

■ *Colons*

The most common use for the colon in business writing is to introduce lists, such as the list of repair centers in the example above. Colons also introduce quotations of more than one sentence, examples to clarify a point, or a thought, word, or phrase that requires a strong introduction. For example:

> Our customer service policy can be described in one word: satisfaction.

■ *Commas*

These little squiggles can wreak more havoc on unsuspecting prose than any other piece of punctuation. They're used more frequently than any other, so their potential for destruction is magnified. But they keep your meaning clear if you use them properly.

Here are a few do's and don'ts to remember when using commas:

- Use commas to join independent clauses (they contain a subject and a verb and express a complete thought) that are linked with conjunctions such as *and, but, or, while, for, nor, yet,* or *so.*

- Use commas to separate items in a series *(like the sentence above).* Whether you use a comma before the last item is a matter of style. News writers shun the penultimate comma; literary writers embrace it. Business writers can do as they like.

- Use commas to separate introductory clauses and long phrases from the main part of the sentence, especially where meaning can be confused without the comma.

  By the time the manager arrived, the warehouse had been flooded.

  Regarding sales, employees work hard to make sure our customers receive the best possible price.

- Use commas to set off clauses and phrases that help explain part of the sentence but aren't essential to its meaning.

  wrong: All employees, who were disrespectful to customers, have been fired. *(Obviously, not all employees were fired; only those who were disrespectful. The phrase is essential to the meaning of the sentence.)*

  right: *All employees who were disrespectful to customers have been fired.*

- Use commas to separate two or more adjectives *only* of you could insert the word *and* between the adjectives.

  She is a conscientious, witty performer. *(conscientious and witty)*

  This is a large Northwest corporation. (*not large and Northwest)*

- Use commas to set off parenthetical information.

  James Brothers, as you know, provides high-quality products at competitive prices.

- Don't use commas before a clause that begins with a subordinating conjunction such as *because, if, since, after, although, before, as, as if, how, when, through, unless, where,* or *while.*

  We will repair your computer at no charge because it is still under warranty.

■ *Dashes and Parentheses*

Both dashes and parentheses can be used to set off information (usually an aside or brief explanation) from the sentence. Be wary of using these devices too frequently or for lengthy clauses within the middle of a sentence. William Faulkner's famous *The Reivers* has a parenthetical insertion that runs on for six pages. By the time you get to the closed parenthesis, you forgot how the sentence began.

When you open a parenthesis, be sure to close it. With dashes, you can either set the phrase within the sentence —with dashes at either side like this—or at the end of the sentence, followed by a period—like this.

■ *Quotation Marks*

Like parentheses, quotation marks need both an opening and a closing. Problems arise when deciding where to put the quotation marks in relation to other punctuation. Here are the rules:

- Periods and commas always go inside the end quotation mark.
- Semicolons and colons always go outside.
- With exclamation points and question marks, it depends on whether they are part of the quoted material.

   Have you seen our pamphlet, "Technical Services"?

   You asked, "How can Base Line sell its products so inexpensively?"

   The new software is called "Publish It!"

■ *Hyphens*

Use hyphens to link words that work together to describe nouns. A *good-natured employee* refers to an employee with a pleasing nature, not to a good employee. The first word, *good,* modifies or describes the base word, *natured,* and together they modify *employee.* When you have two modifiers for the same base word, as in the sentence below, omit the first base word but leave the hyphen, as follows:

   Both one-word and two-word names apply.

   Both one- and two-word names apply.

Don't use hyphens, however, when the first word in a two-word modifier is *very* or an adverb that ends in *-ly*.

■ *Apostrophes*

If you're writing in an informal style, you'll use apostrophes to form contractions—shortened words more like spoken English rather than written text. *You're* is short for *you are*, *isn't* for *is not*, and so forth. The apostrophe stands in for one or more missing letters.

Where some writers become uncertain is with the possessive case of nouns and pronouns. To make a word possessive—to show ownership—you add an apostrophe *s* (*'s*). Here are some quick rules to help sort through the confusion:

- With singular nouns and indefinite pronouns, add *'s* to indicate ownership (*committee's, Joe's, boss's, Charles's, somebody's, one's, everyone's anyone's*).

- With plural nouns that end in *s*, just add the apostrophe (*lawyers' briefs, managers' meeting, secretaries' phones,* but *women's agenda, men's room, children's toys*).

- Remember that the only time you use an apostrophe with a pronoun is to create a contraction. *It's* is the contraction of *it is*. The possessive pronoun is *its*. *Who's* means *who is; whose* is the possessive case.

WATCH FOR COMMON LANGUAGE PITFALLS

Here are a few more common problems that befall even experienced writers. Watch for them in your own writing.

■ *Redundancies*

basic essentials	enter into	plan in advance
blue in color	final conclusion	the reason is because
close proximity	may possibly	right and proper
completely eliminate	mutual agreement	square in shape
consensus of opinion	necessary requirement	three p.m. in the afternoon
end result	original founder	two equal halves

■ *Word Choice*

- You *affect* the result; the result of your actions is the *effect*. (*Occasionally "effect" is used as a verb to mean "make happen," as in "I will effect a change in the procedures."*)

- You are *among* friends, but that's *between* you and me. (*Use among with undefined numbers or relationships; use between with two or when the relationship shared by the parts is clearly defined, as in "negotiations between management, employees, and union leaders."*)

- It looks *as if* my ship has come in, but it looks *like* my ship. (*"As if" is a conjunction that announces a verb clause; "like" is a preposition that can only introduce a noun or pronoun.*)

- *Because* you want to indicate that time has passed, use the word *since*.

- You *compare* one thing *to* another when you emphasize differences; you *compare with* when you look for similarities as well as differences.

- Your lunch is *composed of* a sandwich and an apple; your lunch *comprises (includes, takes in)* all the major food groups.

- The telephone's dial tone is *continuous (unbroken)*; the telephone's ringing off the hook all day causes *continual (repeated, frequent)* interruptions.

- You *differ from* someone if you are unlike each other, but you *differ with* someone when you have a disagreement.

- You're *disinterested* when you are impartial, *uninterested* if you lack interest.

- You'll get *further* in improving your writing if you remember that only *farther* refers to actual physical distance.

- *Fewer* words is an admirable goal; *less* text is the result. (*Use "fewer" when you mean a number of items; use "less" when you refer to a quantity, amount, or period of time.*)

- You *elicit* information when you ask questions; *illicit* means unlawful.

- You *imply* when you speak or write; you *infer* when you read or hear.

- Before you *lie* down, *lay* your spectacles on the night stand. (*The past tense is trickier: Last night she lay down after she laid her spectacles on the table. Also: She was lying down, and she was laying her spectacles on the table.*)

- Your *principal (primary)* concern is to assure all the high *principles (beliefs)* of the company are conveyed in your letter.

- *Who* is used only for people; *that* is used for things or collective nouns that are made up of people *(group, committee)*.

- *Who* you hire depends on *who* has the most experience or with *whom* you were most impressed. (*"Whom" is used only when it is the object of a verb or preposition.*)

■ *Dangling Participles*

Beware the dangling participle, that lovely little phrase that starts a sentence, but then leaves you hanging when the sentence doesn't follow logically. Here are some examples:

- Turning from standard procedures, you have been granted a refund. *(Problem: "You" didn't turn from standard procedure, so "Turning" is left dangling.)*

- Turning from standard procedures, the manager has granted a refund. *(Now "turning" has something to modify: "manager.")*

- Afraid of the consequences, the note was left anonymously. *(Obviously the note wasn't afraid, but the anonymous individual was. Revise by recasting the sentence: The anonymous note was left by someone afraid of the consequences.)*

■ *Prepositions*

Use fewer prepositions and your writing will improve in both clarity and conciseness. Here are a few verbs commonly abused by prepositions; the italicized prepositions can be deleted without loss:

continue *on*	head *up*	slow *up*
cancel *out*	join *up*	spread *out*
distribute *out*	phone *up*	stand *up*
face *up*	refer *back*	return *back*

These are only the basics of punctuation and grammar. Keep a complete reference book handy and consult it when you're unsure. The more you use it, the more the knowledge will become automatic.

Several excellent reference books are available to provide greater detail and explanation for the rules of grammar, punctuation, and style. Some of my favorites are Strunk and White's classic *The Elements of Style*, Sheridan Baker's *The Practical Stylist*, E.D. Johnson's *The Handbook of Good English*, and Duncan McDonald and Lauren Kessler's excellent text, *When Words Collide*.

4

SAMPLE CUSTOMER SERVICE LETTERS

The sample letters presented here come from a broad range of companies—from major chemical manufacturers to book distributors to mail order companies to computer software manufacturers. Some of the companies that contributed letters preferred to remain anonymous, so I have eliminated corporate logos and in many cases have changed the name of the company in respect of that wish. *All addresses and telephone numbers have been changed, and all names of individuals are fictional.* When a letter refers to "the number below" or "the address above," this refers to the phone number and address that are part of the company letterhead.

Some of the letters that follow deal with specific circumstances, sometimes related to a specific industry, but the general structure and language can be adapted for your own letters. Many of the letters are set up as computerized form letters, which allows you to personalize each letter while maintaining the efficiency of the form letter. All are organized according to the specific purpose of the letter. I've also included a few examples of fax and e-mail correspondence.

1 ■ REQUESTING INFORMATION

These are routine letters that ask for information that will enable you to process a customer's request, order, or contract. They need to be specific and ask for all the information you need in a clear and concise manner so that you don't have to go back and ask again. As with many routine letters, these can easily be made into form letters. With the sophisticated word processing programs currently available, it's easy to personalize these as well, even though the contents of the letter will be unchanged.

ASKING FOR INFORMATION NEEDED TO PROCESS CUSTOMER REQUEST

This form letter is set up to take information from a database program or mail list file. Many database programs build in the option of creating letters within the program, allowing you to print a single letter or a series of letters to a number of customers.

[date]

[first name] [last name]
[address]
[city], [state] [zip code]

Re: Account Number [acct. no.]
        Cellular Number [phone no.]

Dear [title] [last name],

I received your request for a name change on your account. In order to complete this request, we require a new subscriber agreement in the name of the party who will now be responsible for that account. I have enclosed a subscriber agreement; please complete it and return it to my attention, along with a number where you can be reached, so that I may review it and call you with a response as quickly as possible. Until we can process your request, the party currently named on the account will remain responsible for any charges incurred.

If you have any questions, please don't hesitate to call.

Sincerely,

Client Service Representative

REQUESTING INFORMATION TO RESOLVE NON-DELIVERY COMPLAINT

This form letter is not set up for mail-merge capabilities. Instead, the customer service representative calls up the original letter, replaces all the "xxxx" entries with the appropriate text, then prints and mails it. In this instance, it's a good idea to do a computer search for x's just to be sure none have been left in the letter.

xxxx xx, 19xx

xxxx
xxxx
xxxx

Dear xxxx:

Recently you informed us that your order of xxxx has not been received. Our records show that the account is currently up-to-date, with neither orders nor payments pending.

Unfortunately, we have been unable to identify an order and payment covering delivery prior to the current order.

Please send full details regarding the total remittance involved and the channels through which you placed the order and made payment. A copy of the original order would be helpful.

Once we have received this information, we will be able to determine whether a shipment was made and begin to trace it. I will also then have the information I need to search further for the missing payment. If all is in order, I will send out a new order immediately.

Thank you for your patience. Please mail or fax the information to my attention as soon as possible; your concern will receive my immediate attention.

Sincerely,

Jay Parker-Howell
Customer Service Representative

FORM LETTER FOR REQUESTING MISSING INFORMATION OR ADVISING ON INCORRECT INFORMATION

This form letter is set up to deal with a number of questions. The customer service representative simply writes in the missing information and checks the numbered item that requires the customer's response.

Date:

Your PO#
Berrett Reference #

Dear Sir or Madam:

We have received your purchase order. We would like to advise you of the following:

___1. F.O.B. shipping point is Columbus, Ohio. Freight charges are prepaid and added to the order. The freight charges on your order amount to $ _____ .

___2. Credit terms are Net 30 days, upon credit review.

___3. Discounts for early payment are not offered.

___4. Your order is being processed. You may expect delivery on

_____ .

___5. Please correct our mailing address with your company. Send purchase orders to: Berrett Industrial, P.O. Box BI, Columbus, OH 43211.

___6. Please correct our Remit to address in your records. Send payments to: Berrett Industrial, 3321 Lake Blvd., Cleveland, OH 43321.

___7. _____

Thank you for your continued interest in Berrett products. We appreciate the opportunity to serve you. If you have any questions, please call our Customer Service Department at 1-800-555-2211.

Sincerely,

Claire Rathbone
Customer Service Manager

REQUESTING INFORMATION ABOUT RETURNED MERCHANDISE

March 15, 1995

Fred Barnes
Georgetown Technical Services
P.O. Box 114
Georgetown, MA 02115

Dear Mr. Barnes:

Thank you for selecting a Symantec product.

Recently, we received a returned product from you. We were unable to locate any written instructions within the package.

In order to process this return in a timely manner, we need additional information. Please complete the enclosed form, or contact the Order Administration Department at Symantec (800-555-1029) to provide the information over the phone. You may also fax the paperwork to 800-555-1103.

Please refer to RMA number SC-22431-44.

I look forward to hearing from you soon.

Sincerely,

Symantec Order Administration

RETURNING CHECK; NO ORDER ENCLOSED

July 12, 1995

Darren Vincent
8933 S.E. Crescent Avenue
San Francisco, CA 90412

Dear Mr. Vincent:

Enclosed, please find a check issued by you or your organization which we recently received. Unfortunately, the check was not accompanied by an order form or an invoice. Therefore, we're unable to apply the funds.

If you'd like to order a product, then please return the enclosed check with an order form or instruction letter and mail it to:

Symantec Corporation
Prepaid Order Processing
175 West Broadway
Eugene, OR 97401

Please remember to include a street address for shipping and proof of ownership if you're ordering a product upgrade (i.e., copy of title page from user manual, program disk, customer ID number, or a copy of your original purchase receipt).

If you would like to make payment against an invoice, please return the enclosed check with a copy of your invoice and mail it to:

Symantec Corporation
Attn: Accounts Payable
10210 Torero Avenue
Cupertino, CA 95014

If you have any questions about this letter, please call Customer Service at (800) 555-1234 or (408) 555-1292.

Thank you.

Customer Service

Enclosure

2 ■ PROVIDING INFORMATION

Customer service frequently involves providing information to customers, sometimes when the customer has specifically requested it, and sometimes when the company needs to let customers know about changes, new services, or other relevant news. These, like letters requesting information, are often repeated to a large number of customers, and therefore form letters make sense.

FORM LETTER RESPONDING TO REQUESTS FOR INFORMATION

Although I advocate personalizing letters when possible, sometimes that's just not efficient. This is especially true when you would not otherwise be entering the individual's name in your customer database. For a company as large as Cellular One, individually addressing every letter that went out in response to information requests would require far more time and expense than any additional benefits that personal responses might justify.

Dear Cellular One Client:

Enclosed please find the information you requested. As part of the nation's largest cellular communications company, we are constantly trying to improve the quality of service we provide for you.

Should you desire further information concerning your service, such as roaming information, updated coverage areas, or a rate analysis, please call us. You may dial 611 from your cellular phone or reach us at one of the numbers below. And remember, we are always here to help you, 24 hours a day.

We look forward to hearing from you soon.

Sincerely,

Client Services Representative

FORWARDING INFORMATION UPON CUSTOMER REQUEST

This is a similar form letter but it is set up as a merge file that allows you to personalize the letter, giving your customer the impression that you sat down and replied as soon as you received the request. It's a very straightforward, simple structure that thanks the customer, provides the information, then leaves with an offer of more help whenever it's needed.

[LETTER DATE]

[CUSTOMER NAME/ADDR]
[ADDRESS LINE 1]
[ADDRESS LINE 2]
[CITY, STATE ZIP]

Dear [SALUTATION]:

Thank you for taking the time to [METHOD DESC] us. We are always interested in hearing from our customers.

We hope the enclosed literature is helpful.

If you have any questions or comments in the future, we would be happy to hear from you.

[USER CLOSING]

[USER NAME]
[USER TITLE]
[USER DEPARTMENT]

[USER INITIALS]
[REF NUMBER]
[CARBON COPIES]

[ENCLOSURES]

WELCOMING A NEW CUSTOMER

Although letters welcoming new customers are routine, this is an example of an easy letter to personalize. You will most likely be adding the customer to your computer database. Most database programs allow you to merge specific data fields with text, so why not just print out a mail-merged letter at the same time?

[date]

[firstname] [lastname]
[title]
[company]
[address1]
[address2]
[city], [state] [zipcode]

Dear [greeting] [lastname]:

It is my great pleasure to welcome you as a new client.

Please note two important promises that Intelleverse makes to all our customers:

• **Guaranteed satisfaction.** If for any reason you are not pleased with one of our products, you will receive either an overnight replacement or refund. The only questions we'll ask are ones to help us make sure you'll be satisfied with your next purchase.

• **24-hour free technical support.** No other company in our industry offers free technical support 24 hours a day. But we're just like you. We're committed to being the best in the business, and that means long hours and hard work. We want to be there when you need us.

I've enclosed some information that you will find helpful in our future relationship—a list of department phone numbers, an order department and procedure card for your Rollodex, and our latest technical support manual.

Please call me if you have any questions or need more information. I'm happy to help any time.

By choosing Intelleverse, you've shown your faith in us. We plan to live up to that trust.

Sincerely,

Candace Harrison, Customer Support Manager

RESPONDING TO A REQUEST FOR PRICING INFORMATION

January 19, 1995

Ms. Susan Calvin
Director of Nursing
Bayview
Box 11246
Boston, MA 02112

Dear Ms. Calvin:

I am pleased to forward to you the enclosed price proposal and product information that you requested.

The prices are in effect through July 1, 1995, and do not include applicable sales tax. Our terms are net 30 days, F.O.B. destination, with delivery taken three months after receipt of order.

Should you have any questions, please feel free to call me at our toll-free Customer Service number, 1-800-555-0112.

Thank you for allowing us to be of service to you.

Sincerely yours,

Archibald MacIver
Assistant Manager, Customer Service

WELCOMING NEW RESIDENT TO TOWN

When working on another book project, I wrote to the local chamber of commerce in a small community in central Oregon. As a result of that request, I received several letters, like the one below, from local businesses welcoming me to the community. I was impressed with the good-will gestures from these companies. In some companies, contacts like this might be handled by the sales department, but customer service operations, as in the case of this bank, might also want to anticipate the needs of potential customers.

October 12, 1995

Cheryl McLean
ImPrint Services
2150 Jackson Creek Drive
Corvallis, Oregon 97330

Dear Cheryl:

The Chamber of Commerce has informed us of your interest in our area.

We would like to welcome you to the community and invite you into the Prineville branch of the Bank of Central Oregon. We live in a special community and look forward to helping you settle in. I am enclosing a brochure of our services, and if we can be of help, please let us know.

Sincerely,

Tamar Braly
Operations Supervisor

Encl.

FOLLOW-UP OF PHONE CONVERSATION, PROVIDING INFORMATION

March 24, 1995

Joseph Morris
11243 Wanetka Lane
Sunrise, FL 33325

Dear Mr. Morris:

Thank you for your call on October 11. In response to your request, Drew Manufacturing is the original producer of the item you inquired about, the DR 3000 monometer, item #32105-332. We have no authorized distributors for this product.

If you need specification sheets or anything else about the DR 3000, please contact our Miami Customer Service Department at 1-800-555-1119.

Thank you for your interest in Drew products.

Sincerely,

Drew Manufacturing
Customer Service

NOTIFYING CUSTOMERS OF PRICE INCREASE

This letter announces price increases in a way that expresses the company's reluctance and appreciation for the customer's understanding.

January 26, 1994

Dear Interstate Oil Company Distributors:

OPEC is at it again! The shifting policies of the Middle East oil cartel has once again thrown the American market into instability.

Unfortunately, what that means for us is the immediate need to increase prices on both number one and number two grade home heating oils. As of March 1, per gallon prices will increase from 56¢ to 72¢ for number one oil, and from 48¢ to 60¢ for number two oil. The larger percentage increase for number two oil results from limited domestic refinery production and an increasing inability to acquire foreign products.

We appreciate your understanding. We know that you appreciate that in the current marketplace, we can't always manage to keep prices as low as we would like them to stay. We believe this to be a temporary measure, however, and you can count on us to be even faster at reducing the prices than we've been at having to raise them.

Please call me if you have any questions or need assistance in implementing the price increase in your territory.

Sincerely,

Bob Wilson
Distribution

INFORMING CUSTOMERS OF CHANGE IN RETURNS POLICY

It's difficult to put a positive spin on the news when a policy change affects your customers in a negative way. This letter focuses on how overly generous the previous policy was and that the change simply brings the company into line with the competition.

April 17, 1995

Dear Publisher:

As we all know, higher profits and lower administrative costs are every company's goals in the nineties. Because of this, it has become necessary for Books International to rework its returns procedures for publishers, and I ask you for your cooperation.

In the past our policy has been that you could send books back to us that were damaged or shopworn and not accept them as part of the return. We even paid the freight. You'll admit that, in this industry, that was an overly lenient policy on our part, particularly since we bought the books from you on a fully returnable basis.

The fact is, we accept returns from bookstores that are shopworn, in the spirit of customer service. Therefore, we are asking you to accept all the books we return to you. As of June 1, 1995, we can no longer accept refused returns or pay the freight-back charges. Furthermore, in most cases we are no longer able to sort through our customer returns to determine which books we can resell and which books we can't, so we will be sending you all customer returns, instead of putting the books back into our inventory.

If you wish to discuss our new policy, please call the buyer who handles your account. If there is a problem with a particular title or item in a return shipment, please feel free to call our Accounts Payable department. We are sorry for any inconvenience, and hope that you understand this was a necessary change.

Sincerely,

Catherine Newstrom
Vice-President, Publisher Relations

SENDING INFORMATION SHEETS AND DISTRIBUTION INFORMATION

February 15, 1995

Terra Lindsey
City Manager
Box 11250
Beaumont, TX 77704

Dear Ms. Lindsey:

Thank you for your telephone call yesterday. I have located the information you requested and have enclosed the specification sheets for the TM350 model water meter, the JC560 hose adapters, and the PT55 tubes.

Each of these products can be purchased from any of our authorized distributors, a list of which is enclosed. The RC560 pipes, however, can be ordered directly from our central warehouse in Atlanta at 1-800-555-0211. We have no authorized distributors for this product.

If you need additional specification sheets or anything else regarding these or other Pemco products, please call our central Customer Service Department at 1-800-555-2211.

Thank you for your continued interest in Pemco products. We look forward to serving you.

Sincerely,

Pamela Briney
Customer Service Manager
Central Region

Enclosures

INFORMING CUSTOMERS OF CHANGE OF ADDRESS/ORDER PROCEDURE

January 15, 1995

Dear Pimlico Customer:

We recently received your purchase order, number   at our regional office in Bangor, Maine. That office is now being used only for instrument repairs. All mail is being forwarded to our world headquarters in Boston. We apologize for the delay that occurred in processing your order, but have expedited shipping procedures to prevent further delay.

We would appreciate your help by sending future written correspondence as follows:

Purchase Orders to: All other correspondence to:

Pimlico International   Pimlico International
P.O. Box PI   P.O. Box PI
Savannah, GA 31412   Boston, MA 02114

Your help in forwarding correspondence to the appropriate address will enable us to provide you with the best customer service possible. If you should have any questions concerning orders, or any of our products, please call us at 1-800-555-4431.

Thank you for your continued interest in Pimlico. Your business, as always, is greatly appreciated.

Yours sincerely,

Vern Russell
Vice President for Customer Relations

Notifying New Client of Account Number and Order Procedures

New customers deserve a special note of thanks, particularly when they show signs of being very good customers indeed. This letter welcomes the new customer, thanks her for a large order, and provides information that will help her place orders in the future.

March 26, 1995

Cathy Dellaren
City Administrator
City of Brownsville
400 Main Street
Brownsville, IN 47325

Dear Cathy,

I enjoyed talking with you yesterday and appreciate the sizable order you've placed for Pimlico products for the City of Brownsville. We're delighted to have you as a new customer.

Your order is being processed, and our technical crew will contact you soon with delivery and installation schedules.

Your account number with Pimlico is G-445-223-1. We ask that you use this number each time you place an order. To make this easier for you, I've enclosed a Rolodex card with our order number, customer service number, and your account number. By using your account number when you order, we can provide the best possible customer service.

Also, could you please confirm the appropriate contact person in your purchasing department for our records.

Thank you for your assistance. We look forward to serving you again soon.

Best regards,

Drew Johnson
New Customer Support Manager

SENDING PRICE QUOTATION

Sending pricing information often falls under the responsibility of the customer service staff rather than the sales staff. This letter spells out the terms and several benefits of ordering with this company.

April 15, 1995

Margaret Velazquez
Pullman Water & Sewer Authority
P.O. Box 4431
Pullman, AZ 85123

Dear Margaret,

On behalf of ChemField, thank you for your consideration of our products for your use. In order to assure quoted prices are honored at the time your order is placed, or if you have questions with respect to this quotation, please refer to the Quotation Number Q94842.

Your contract would be renewable for a one-year period with the option of price increases. ChemField would notify of price increase within thirty days of the renewal date.

The ChemField Company is a direct seller and distributor of its own American-manufactured instruments, accessories, and chemical reagents. We take great care to provide our customers with outstanding value in the quality of products and services we provide at very competitive prices. We have not priced our products for multi-level distribution channels so that we might more effectively serve our loyal customers.

Should you need additional information, please contact me directly at 800-555-1124, extension 32.

Yours sincerely,

Barbara Askenzi
Customer Service Representative

NOTIFYING CUSTOMERS OF PRICE CHANGES

This letter gives both good news and bad news—some prices have increased, others have decreased. Note how giving the bad news first allows the letter to end on a positive note with the good news about lower prices.

April 21, 1995

Dear Varnelli Customers:

The new price schedule for Varnelli products is enclosed. We want to point out that while many prices have increased, others have actually gone down.

The bad news first: Due to import tax increases and greater restrictions on goods, we've had no choice but to increase the prices on imported products from the East. Prices themselves, regardless of the increased tariffs, have increased beyond what we could continue to absorb. Until only recently we've managed to keep prices low by depleting existing inventory.

Now for some good news: Imports from Mexico and Latin America have enjoyed reduced tariffs. Also, we've opened an office in Mexico City that enables us to seek out the best deals on the highest quality merchandise. We know you'll be pleased with the greater selection and increased quality—not to mention the lower prices!

Please call our customer service line if you have any questions or concerns. We're available daily from 7 a.m. to 7 p.m. Pacific Time. We look forward to hearing from you.

Sincerely,

Margie Weston
Distribution and Customer Service Manager

FACSIMILE RESPONDING TO REQUEST FOR PRICING

This facsimile responds to the customer's request but asks for additional information that the customer left out.

May 23, 1995

TRANSMITTED BY FAX

TO: Joan Lawrence
         Peninsula Railroad Company
         Fax: 434-555-1235

FROM: Penny Miller
         ChemField Customer Service Department
         Phone: 800-555-3984; Fax: 332-555-0984

SUBJECT: Price quotation request dated 5-23-95

Dear Ms. Lawrence,

Thank you for your interest in ChemField products. In response to your fax request, which I received this morning, I have attached a quotation for your consideration.

I have quoted items listing catalog part numbers, but I am unable to quote some items due to a lack of part numbers. If you would like to identify which parts you were requesting from the catalog, I will add these to the quotation.

We will honor these prices for a period of one year, if you decide to turn this into a priced blanket order.

Please note that our terms for shipping are FOB–Crawfordsville, Indiana. We prepay shipping, then add it to your invoice. We cannot quote shipping charges until we have the specific order.

If you have any questions, please call me. I'm looking forward to making sure you get the service you need from ChemField.

Sincerely,

Tanya Garvey
Customer Service Representative

INFORMING CUSTOMERS OF NEW OPTIONS FOR PLACING ORDERS AND RETRIEVING INFORMATION

This form letter is not individualized because it is going to all of the company's customers. The enthusiastic tone of this letter is bound to carry over to those customers who can take advantage of the new service. Notice that the letter asks for feedback—this is a way to test the interest in this new service. A postscript can be an effective attention-getter, but it shouldn't be used as an after thought. The postscript draws the reader's eye and is best used to emphasize a point or make a request or suggest the desired customer response.

June 16, 1995

Dear Priceline Customers:

Priceline has joined the Electronic Age! We are excited to offer our Priceline customers who have already connected to the information superhighway easy access to Priceline customer service and support.

You can also browse through our multimedia on-line catalog through the World Wide Web.

For those of you with FAX machines, you can call our automated information request number—toll-free—to get full product information by return facsimile.

Finally, because we realize that many of us prefer contact with a real person, our customer service staff are available by phone to respond to your questions or help solve any problems you may have encountered.

Please use the attached Rollodex card to keep all our access options at your fingertips:
- Direct Customer Service toll-free phone 1-800-555-1002
- Automated Fax-Info line 1-800-555-0021
- E-mail addresses
  Customer Service Service@priceline.com
  Order Department Order@princeline.com
  Technical Support Tech@priceline.com
- World Wide Web //http/priceline/www

We're looking forward to serving you by whichever medium you choose.

Sincerely,

Josh Harrison
Director, Customer Service

P.S. Next time you're on line, drop me a quick e-mail message. I'm eager to make connections with our customers on the information superhighway!

PROVIDING PRODUCT AND ORDER INFORMATION IN RESPONSE TO INQUIRY

October 30, 1995

Pamela Barger
4335 West Lafayette
Summitville, IN 46070

Dear Ms. Barger:

Thank you for your recent request for information on cross-grading your Symantec software. We apologize for the delay of this response.

For registered users, the cost to cross-grade to Norton Utilities for the Mac version 3.1 is $39.95 plus $8 shipping and handling, as well as any applicable tax.

If you are not currently registered, we accept any of the following as proof of ownership: a serial number; a copy of your sales receipt; a copy of the title page of your manual; or a copy of the front of your program disk.

To place an order, or for additional information about Symantec products and services, please call our Customer Service Department at (800)

555-2233 or, if you prefer, you may fax an order to (503) 555-3344.

Orders may also be mailed to:

> Symantec Corporation
> Attention Prepaid Order Processing
> P.O. Box 10849
> Eugene, OR 97440

With your order, please specify the disk size (3.5" or 5.25") and a street address for shipping. For credit card orders, we accept Visa, MasterCard, and American Express. When placing an order by credit card please include the expiration date.

Again, thank you for your interest in Symantec products. We look forward to being of service to you again in the future.

Sincerely,

Barrie Cannaletto
Customer Service

3 ■ Expressing Thanks

Saying a simple "thank you" is one of the most commonly overlooked opportunities to remind your customers of what a great company you are. Sometimes a quick note on the back of a postcard or a post-it note attached to an order confirmation are all that you need to bring a smile to your customer's face.

There are plenty of times when a brief note of thanks is appropriate: orders, letters of inquiry, and comments or suggestions, whether positive or negative. You can use this as a way to provide information or clarify company goals or commitments. Either way, it's a small effort with often big payoffs. Get in the "thank you" habit!

SAYING THANKS TO A CUSTOMER WHO HELPED OUT

Sometimes we develop relationships with customers that allow us to ask favors. It's best when, as in the case below, the favor is also a feather in the cap to the customer, but even simple favors—such as letting you know about a rumor that might hurt your business or passing along the name of a reliable supplier—deserve a special note of thanks. If your handwriting is legible, sometimes a simple handwritten note can be most personal and therefore most effective. In this case, when the salutation is made on a first-name basis, the writer would sign his first name only, even though the typed form calls for the full name to be at the closing. Note that, in such a personal letter, the writer's title can be omitted.

September 1, 1995

John Ashcroft
General Manager
Portland Technical Services
Suite 1128
332 East Burnside
Portland, Oregon 97201

Dear John,

Your presentation at the Rotary Club was inspired—and inspirational. I know several members who walked away geared up for improving their business planning.

You've always been an important customer at Centech, and I knew that with your business acumen and experience you would have a lot to offer at the business development program. I want to thank you again for responding to my plea with such generosity.

Please be my guest for lunch the next time you're in town. I'm looking forward to a chance to talk with you further about your presentation. You gave me some very intriguing ideas!

Again, please accept my very sincere thanks.

With best regards,

Stu Valley

THANKING CUSTOMERS FOR THEIR BUSINESS

September 24, 1995

Dear friends,

I glanced at my calendar this morning and realized that it was only three years ago today that my partner and I launched Custom Mechanics in my garage at home. What a difference three years can make!

Today, Custom Mechanics has 54 highly trained professionals in three locations in the state. And we're getting ready to move into Wisconsin and Minnesota in January.

We couldn't have done it without your support and confidence. We felt it was time to stop and say thanks for being our customer!

Best regards,

Will Cawley & Steve Brabent
General Managers

APPRECIATION FOR MEMBERSHIP APPLICATION

This form letter allows you to send a quick, courteous thank you to new life-time members whose significant contribution or payment entitles them to a personalized response. The data fields allow for the letter to be addressed to an individual or a company representative, as appropriate.

[date]

[firstname] [lastname]
[title]
[company]
[address1]
[address2]
[city], [state] [zipcode]

Dear [greeting] [lastname]:

The Quill Literary Society thanks you for your application and remittance for life membership. We are privileged to have you permanently affiliated with the Society.

As a Life Member you will enjoy the satisfaction of being a lifelong sponsor of the Society's educational and scientific research. And, of course, you will receive your copy of Quill Literary magazine every month without ever having to renew your membership.

Your Life Membership Certificate is now being prepared and will be mailed to you shortly. In the meantime, let me be the first to officially welcome you as our newest Life Member.

Sincerely yours,

Paula M. Meierman
Manager, Customer Service

THANKING FOR MEMBERSHIP AND OFFERING SPECIAL GIFT

Sometimes you will want your appreciation to take a tangible form. This letter expresses appreciation and offers a reward for the customer's loyalty. This form letter is set up to be filled in individually rather than grouped with identical as part of a larger mail merge.

xxxx, 19xx

xxxx
xxxx
xxxx

Dear xxxx:

Thank you for your letter extending your membership in the Pinnacle Opera Association.

It is a source of great pride to us that your membership has extended for a period of so many years. Needless to say, it is through the interest and loyalty of members such as yourself that the Association has attained the prominent position it now enjoys in our community, state, and region.

In recognition of your long continued affiliation, we take pleasure in enclosing these tickets for the Opera Association special event of your choice. These are events outside the usual opera season and not covered by your season tickets. The enclosed calendar outlines the performances, and we are delighted by the diversity of offerings.

We hope you will enjoy the performance of your choice as our guests. Thank you again for your loyal support.

Yours sincerely,

Megan Wainright
Member Services

FORM LETTER THANKING CUSTOMER FOR COMMENTS

Notice that this letter simply says thank you for making comments, it doesn't dwell on whether they were positive or negative. It doesn't hurt to acknowledge the good or bad slant of the customer's comments, but the subtle modesty of this letter has a different appeal.

todaydate

name *lastname*
company
address
city, *state* *zip*

Dear *title* *lastname*:

Thank you so much for your recent comments about our products and services.

We consider customer feedback extremely valuable to the success of our products and our business. We appreciate your taking the time to share your thoughts with us.

All product and service comments are forwarded to the appropriate departments and groups for their review and evaluation.

Thanks for letting us know how you feel!

Sincerely,

Janet Harrison
Manager, Customer Service

THANKING CUSTOMER FOR CHANGE-OF-ADDRESS NOTICE

The primary purpose of this letter is to get additional information, but the message the customer receives is one of appreciation for her thoughtfulness. The request for the additional information seems like an aside rather than the central message.

August 16, 1995

Melinda Treever
Visalia Industrial Supply
P. O. Box 4433
Visalia, CA 98021

Dear Ms. Treever:

Thank you for taking the time to inform us of your new address. Power Mechanicals Inc. is committed to providing quality customer service, and your help toward that goal is always appreciated.

In order for PMI to maintain accurate and complete customer information, we would appreciate your help in providing a street address for delivery information, as deliveries cannot be shipped to a post office box. I have enclosed a postage-paid reply card for your convenience.

If you have any questions, please call 800-555-1310 and ask for Customer Service. I'll be glad to talk with you.

Thank you again for your time and cooperation.

Best regards,

Anna Vaars
Customer Service

FOLLOW-UP THANKS FOR MEETING

Whenever you've met with a customer or had a discussion in which decisions were made, it's good practice to follow-up with a letter that both thanks the customer for the time spent and confirms the details of the discussion.

January 22, 1995

Stuart Hill
Assistant Manager
Torrence Valley Equipment, Inc.
22 Railroad Way
Torrence, CA 95012

Dear Stuart:

Thank you for taking the time to meet with us yesterday to help us understand your specific requirements. We enjoyed the chance to get down to details in a way that will enable us to provide precisely the products and services you need.

As Customer Support Manager, I will coordinate schedules and maintain regular contact to be sure we stay on track. Briefly, here is the schedule we've worked out for the current project.

- Design phase begins February 1
- Trial runs begin March 15
- Evaluation meetings held March 29-30 with design team and representatives from Torrence Valley Equipment
- Implementation target date: April 30

Our engineering staff will work hard to assure that only one round of trials will be needed, but the schedule includes some flex time for unforeseen problems or delays. If you have any further thoughts about your requirements, or questions about the proposed schedule, please call me.

We're excited to be working with Torrence on this project. It's for jobs like this that we all got into this business. We appreciate the opportunity to work with you.

Sincerely,

Jane Meadows
Customer Support Manager

4 ■ Expressing Compliments

Opportunities to give your customers compliments are not as common as the chance to say thanks, but they pack a lot of power for good will. Some examples of situations that allow you to compliment your clients are promotions, retirements, weddings, births, honors and awards, or any new development. The tone of such letters is generally personal and friendly.

CONGRATULATING CUSTOMER ON RECENT AWARD

September 9, 1995

Mr. John Webber, President
Data Reproductions, Inc.
One S.W. Claymore
San Francisco, California 94015

Dear John,

Congratulations on being selected Volunteer of the Month in your community. I read about the award in the business pages and was very impressed by your commitment. I was proud to show the article to our staff and say—this is one of our best customers!

Thanks for all you do, both for your community and for your loyalty as a customer. We appreciate the opportunity to help your business stay on top.

Best regards,

Mina Saluzik
Vice President, Client Relations

CONGRATULATIONS ON RETIREMENT

October 12, 1995

Catherine Marrioni
Assistant Vice President
Teledyne International
23419 West Highway 64
Harrisburg, PA 17121

Dear Catherine,

We want to extend our sincere best wishes for your retirement. You have been a valued customer for many years, and we're going to miss you!

We have appreciated your support over the years. Our growth in the last decade is due to loyal customers like you. We wish you some well-deserved R&R.

Sincerely,

Rob Philips
Director, Customer Services

5 ■ REFUSING CUSTOMER REQUESTS

When the customer wants something you can't provide, your tact and diplomacy in letter-writing face a special challenge. You have to say no, but you can say it with a smile—even in writing. Here are several examples that get the negative message across in a way that keeps the relationship with the customer on a positive note.

APOLOGY FOR DELAYED RESPONSE/INABILITY TO HELP

This letter is being sent by facsimile to expedite the response, which is already delayed. It opens with a gracious thanks for an invitation to speak at a stockholders meeting, then explains the reason for both the delayed response and the refusal of the invitation. Acknowledging that she has something to lose by refusing helps soften the refusal, as does the offer to suggest an alternative speaker. The letter closes again with a note of thanks.

July 15, 1995

FAX TO:　　Cheryl Swanson

FROM:　　　Sara Engelbritt

SUBJECT:　　Stockholders meeting

. . . .

Dear Cheryl:

I was flattered and delighted to receive your invitation to speak at your next stockholders meeting. I appreciate your confidence that I would add something to the occasion, and I apologize for not responding to your kind invitation more quickly. Our department recently went through a major expansion and reorganization, which affected me for more than two months. Consequently, my responses to important requests such as yours have been delayed.

Because of the reorganization and its demands on my time, I will not be able to make a presentation at your meeting. I realize this is my loss as well.

Please call me if you would like me to suggest an alternate speaker. I wish you the best in your preparations and look forward to the opportunity to attend future meetings.

Sincerely,

Sara Engelbritt

REFUSING REFUND ON TAX; EXPLAINING TAX LAWS

June 12, 1995

Gloria Woodlawn
10 West Queen Street
San Luis Obispo, CA 94132

Dear Ms. Woodlawn:

Thank you for your letter requesting a credit for the cost of the local tax on your recent order.

We are happy to provide you with an explanation regarding the tax applicable for California residents on orders for material published by the Quill Literary Society.

The Society is required by the state to collect the tax because of advertising offices maintained in San Francisco and Los Angeles. The presence of these offices has been deemed sufficient to have prompted considerable publication business, thereby warranting the tax in question.

The tax is, of course, assessed and collected in accordance with the California State Board of equalization. It is assessed on the base value of an order, including postage and handling, but excluding any special mail service charges — air mail, registered, etc.

We are complying with the State of California regulations and any further questions concerning the matter should be directed to the California State Board of Equalization at (555) 555-2354.

Your interest is appreciated and we hope this information is helpful.

Sincerely yours,

Manager, Customer Service

REFUSING REQUEST FOR SPECIAL MAILING

This letter tactfully explains that the request can't be honored without additional compensation from the reader. The concern is acknowledged, the alternatives are provided that allow the customer to choose the best option.

[date]

[firstname] [lastname]
[address2]
[city], [state] [zipcode]

Dear [greeting] [lastname]:

Thank you for your interest in having our magazine sent to you by special mail. We would like to take this opportunity to provide the following information.

Subscription rates provide for monthly delivery of the magazine by surface mail. Although the magazine mails the issues well in advance of the month for which each issue is due, we have no control over the handling of our magazine once it is released by the Postal Service. If magazines are not received, we are always happy to provide replacements of missing issues at no charge if we are notified before our inventory becomes depleted.

Arrangements for special mailing can be made upon receipt of specific instructions and a payment that covers the additional expense. Air mail will speed delivery and costs $2.90 per issue for delivery to your region in addition to the regular subscription rate.

Some people prefer to receive the magazine by registered surface mail, which generally assures safe receipt. A registered package can be traced through the Postal Service if it fails to arrive. The registration fee is $4.40 per issue or $52.80 per year in addition to the regular subscription rate.

Upon request, we can provide delivery of our magazine by registered mail three times a year in packages of four issues for $4.40 per package or $13.20 per year. Although this method of delivery is less expensive, most people prefer to receive their magazines on a monthly basis.

I hope this information helps you determine which option you prefer. Please call our subscription office at 1-800-555-0011 with your instructions or any further questions you might have. Thank you for your interest in our magazine.

Sincerely,

Customer Service Representative

EXPLAINING CUSTOMER MISUNDERSTANDING OF WARRANTY

This letter responds to a customer who demanded that the company honor an expired warranty. It begins with a note of thanks, then explains the terms of the warranty in a straightforward manner. The letter mentions the extended warranty protection without blaming the customer for not purchasing it sooner.

March 30, 1995

Mr. Jonathan Kelso
P.O. Box 3321
Miami Beach, FL 33139

Dear Mr. Kelso:

Thank you for your call yesterday about your television warranty. I appreciate the opportunity to clarify the terms of the warranty.

All televisions are sold with a one-year parts and labor warranty on all but the picture tube. The tube itself has a two-year warranty. Because it has been 18 months since your purchased your set, and the problem is not with the picture tube, the warranty does not cover the cost of repairs.

We do offer an extended warranty protection, which would be available to cover any future problems you might encounter. Meanwhile, as an authorized service center, we offer repairs at very competitive prices. We would appreciate the opportunity to get your set working perfectly.

I have enclosed a copy of your warranty, as well as information about our extended protection program. If you need more information, or would like us to pick up your set for repairs, just give me a call at 555-2223. I look forward to talking with you.

Sincerely,

Jean Samuels
EQL Repair Center

CORRECTING MISINFORMATION

Sometimes employees make statements that are misinterpreted by the customer or that are incorrect or misleading. The simplest response is to treat it as a misunderstanding or miscommunication. That way you don't suggest the customer is at fault—nor do you accept the responsibility that one of your representatives made a promise that you as a company had no intention of fulfilling. You can avoid such problems by quickly providing correct information.

August 12, 1995

Mrs. Carolyn Fielder
2228 S. Fremont Ave.
Sunrise, Florida 33325

Dear Mrs. Fielder:

Thank you for your letter of October 1, which explained that our telephone sales person guaranteed that your subscription rate would never increase. We apologize for this miscommunication and understand why you would be upset to see an increase on your latest invoice. I have credited your account with the amount you would have had to pay for the increased subscription rate, so your rate will not increase until November 5, 1996.

Because the cost of producing our newspapers is constantly increasing, it would be impossible to guarantee that we would never increase our subscription rates.

We apologize once again for the misunderstanding and hope this action will show our commitment to our customers. We appreciate the opportunity to serve you.

Sincerely,

Steven Henderson
Customer Service Manager

INFORMING CUSTOMER THAT A PRODUCT IS NO LONGER AVAILABLE

When you can't provide the product your customer wants, go to the extra effort to suggest alternatives or find someone who will be able to help meet the customer's needs

June 12, 1995

Todd Walprin
Mobile County Utilities
PO Box 3334-A
Mobile, AL 36421

Dear Mr. Walprin,

Thank you for your call yesterday regarding our product number 3322-11 (5-hp motor assembly). I'm sorry to say that this product is no longer available. Please accept my apologies for any inconvenience you experienced in trying to order a product that has been classed obsolete.

I have asked Ron Abraham of the Technical Services Section to call you to determine the replacement motor assembly that will best serve your needs.

If I can be of further assistance, please call me at 1-800-555-2012. Thank you for your continued interest in our products.

Sincerely,

Sara Valhouk
Customer Service Representative

REFUSING SPECIAL REQUESTS FOR ORDER PROCESSING

When the customer wants a service that is unreasonable, the response letter, like the one below, needs to be direct and firm. The letter explains the customer's responsibilities and the limits of the contract but with a note of appreciation as well as a concession to another, more reasonable, request.

August 15, 1995

Haverford Power & Electric Company
Fall City Power Station
Fall City, VA 23021
Attention: Mr. Joss Clemer

Dear Joss:

Thank you for your blanket order # FF3-22351 for laboratory chemicals and equipment.

I would like to address some issues on the contract. ChemField is unable to monitor total expenditures against a given purchase order. It is the responsibility of the buyer to monitor the dollar amount purchased to ascertain the dollar limit is not exceeded.

Your contract states that a signed delivery ticket must accompany the invoice for payment. ChemField uses UPS or RPS delivery services, which you've requested as the carrier, and we do not have a log of each delivery. If we needed to
provide information for a missing shipment, we could certainly provide this, but it is not standard practice for each order.

I have contacted our shipping department and will have them route your orders as you have requested.

Please call me if you encounter any problems. My number is 800-555-1124, ext. 443. Thank you again for your order.

Sincerely,

Orrin Weber
Customer Service

EXPLAINING THAT DISCOUNTED PRICES DO NOT APPLY TO THE CUSTOMER'S ORDER

June 23, 1995

PPS Energy Inc.
P.O. Box 1193
Terre Haute, IN 47883

Attn: A.L. Reaman

Thank you for your recent blanket order #B11947-22. We have noticed that on your blanket order you show these at discounted prices due to the quantity that you anticipate using throughout the length of the contract. Because the quantity discounts are based on the savings that occur when we do not have to break up prepackaged units, these discounts apply only on a per-shipment basis.

I have repriced the products on this order according to the pricing quoted, which we will honor for one year on the enclosed quote #Q8847.

For future orders, please note that quantity discounts will be offered as follows:

Lots of 10 receive a 10% discount
Lots of 50 receive a 15 % discount

If you have any questions, please call me at 1-800-555-1023, extension 222.

Sincerely yours,

Dean Browning
Customer Service Associate

INFORMING CUSTOMER THAT RETURN REQUEST HAS EXPIRED

This letter anticipates a problem before it arises. The form letter follows up on distributors who had requested authorization to return merchandise but who failed to do so within the specified time limit. The no-nonsense tone of the letter suggests that there will be no compromise. While this is appropriate within the industry, from one business concern to another, the tone in a letter to an individual customer might include a note of appreciation or an acknowledgment that not having returned the product meant that the customer was satisfied after all.

todaydate

name *lastname*
company
address
city, *state* *zip*

Dear *title* *lastname*:

On *reqdate* we issued a return merchandise authorization (RMA) number. This number is now over 60 days without return of a product. As per arrangement with your Symantec Distribution Sales Manager, this RMA has been canceled effective *shipdate*.

Any product returned against this RMA # will be refused and returned to you at your expense. If you have any questions, please contact your Distribution Sales Manager.

Than k you,

Order Administration

DENYING REQUEST AND OFFERING SOLUTION

When you have to deny a request, whenever possible offer an alternative solution that will give the customer another option besides dissatisfaction. Here, although the company can't provide the request free of charge, the letter gives the customer the option of purchasing the requested product.

September 1, 1995

Warren Sanford
P.O. Box 325B
Dallas, TX 76012

Dear Mr. Sanford:

This letter is in response to your request for an additional set of manuals for your software. We will be happy to provide you with a second set of manuals; however, as we only sell one-time replacements, if this manual were to be lost or stolen, we would not be able to provide you with an additional set.

Replacement manuals are available to all registered users of our products. The cost is $25 plus any applicable tax and $8 for shipping and handling.

To place an order, or if you would like additional information or assistance, please feel free to contact us by phone at 800-555-4195 or, if you prefer, we may be reached by fax at 708-555-0133. Please provide a charge card number and expiration date for telephone or fax orders.

Orders may also be mailed to:
     Express Software, Inc.
     Attn: Prepaid Order Processing
     P.O. Box 8492
     Lincolnwood, IL 60611

Thank you for your inquiry. We look forward to being of service to you again in the future.

Sincerely,

Toni LaMadrone
Customer Service

6 ■ GRANTING CUSTOMER REQUESTS

These are the easy letters, the ones that say, "Sure, I'm happy to give you what you want." But sometimes even these letters have to compromise a bit: "I'm delighted to give you what you want, but to do so, I need something from you." Getting that assistance from your customer in a way that maintains your good relationship can sometimes be challenging.

FORWARDING REQUESTED PURCHASE RECEIPT

This form letter, set up for mail-merge, answers a common request for a receipt. Notice that the letter doesn't simply provide the requested information, it takes the opportunity to thank the customer for choosing this company's products.

todaydate

name *lastname*
company
address
city, *state* *zip*

Dear *title* *lastname*:

Thank you for your recent order. Enclosed is the receipt you requested on your recent software purchase. We hope this information is sufficient in the event you need to obtain reimbursement from your company.

Should you need further assistance, please feel free to contact our Customer Service department at (800) 555-6363 or by fax at (580) 555-9373.

Thank you for continuing to support Symantec products. We look forward to serving you again in the future.

Sincerely,

representative
Customer Service

Enclosure

AUTHORIZING SUPPLIER TO ACCEPT RETURNED MERCHANDISE

5/23/95

Mr. John Whitaker
Belmont Distributing
1984 South Veranda Avenue
Annapolis, MD 21408

RE: Customer No. 1988421

Dear Mr. Whitaker:

Thank you for your inquiry about returning our products sent to you by your customers. This letter serves as authorization to return the following Zenon products:

Zenon Systems 5000
Zenon 2509x

The return-of-merchandise authorization form enclosed requires only a few brief notes from you to enable us to process the return and apply the appropriate credit to your account. We especially appreciate knowing the reason for the return, as this helps us—and you—anticipate future problems and deal with them before they happen.

The form also includes labels for you to apply to the shipping boxes. Just call UPS when you're ready for them to be picked up. If you have any questions at all, please feel free to contact Susan Farris at 502-555-1094.

Sincerely,

Customer Service

cc: OA/Distribution

AUTHORIZING CREDIT FOR DIFFERENCE IN PRICING FROM COMPETITOR

This letter grants the request on condition the customer provides written information to substantiate her claim that the competitive price was lower. The letter also takes the opportunity to remind the customer of the quality and commitment to customer service that she enjoys with this company.

June 23, 1995

Kara Phelps, Printing Buyer
Catalogue Productions, Inc.
Rt. 2 Box 142
Reno, NV 89502

Dear Kara,

I appreciate your letter pointing out that your recent printing job with us could have been done less expensively elsewhere.

While I firmly believe that you would not have found the same high quality elsewhere—or the same commitment to customer satisfaction—I will work with you to meet competitive pricing on this and forthcoming jobs.

In order to proceed with a credit authorization, I will need the written bid from the competitor, showing that the bid specifications were the same as those we provided. This helps assure that we're not comparing apples and oranges. A different paper, for example, can affect the cost of a print job like this one as much as 25 percent. For your convenience, you can fax the competitor's bid to 702/555-1203.

We value the business you bring to Jameson Brothers Printing. We look forward to continuing our relationship with Catalogue Productions long into the future.

If you have any questions about this authorization, please call me directly.

Best regards,

Juan A. Guttierez

AGREEING TO CANCEL THE INVOICE ON PRODUCT THAT WAS NOT DELIVERED

Agreeing to a customer's request often requires an apology for the problem that prompted the request in the first place. This letter also begins with a statement of appreciation for the customer's having written.

February 28, 1995

Frederick G. Mitchum
Star Route 3, Box 54213
Topeka, KS 66611

Dear Mr. Mitchum:

Thank you for your recent letter. As you requested, I have rescinded the invoice for your order, number 62115. The order shipped on February 26 because of a late delivery to our warehouse from the manufacturer. I understand that you needed delivery before the 15th of the month.

The order is currently on its way to you. Unfortunately, I cannot cancel delivery. When it arrives, simply refuse it and mark it "Return to Sender." We will cover all costs of shipping, and your invoice will receive final cancellation.

I apologize for any inconvenience you experienced. Please know that this was an unusual circumstance; we hope to have an opportunity to give you our usually prompt, efficient service in the future.

Sincerely,

Wade Anderson
Customer Service Associate

ACCEPTING THE COST FOR SHIPPING ON PRODUCT REPAIR

April 15, 1995

Mr. Kenneth McDougall
Program Manager
West One Supplies, Inc.
Suite 115, Birkman Plaza Building
First and Main
Detroit, Michigan 48221

Dear Kenneth,

Thanks for your call about our invoice to you for equipment repairs. You're absolutely right! We promised to cover all shipping costs for repairs for the first three years, and your equipment is still under that agreement.

I've enclosed a credit statement showing the shipping costs deducted from the amount due. I apologize for the inconvenience. I'm not sure how the error occurred, but we'll work to make sure it doesn't happen again. Thank you for catching it!

Let me know if you have any questions. My direct number is 313-555-0312.

Sincerely,

Ben Shipman
Manager, Customer Service

PROVIDING COMPENSATION FOR POOR SERVICE

When a customer has a bad experience with your products or services, the situation sometimes requires more than a simple apology. In this instance, an airline company has provided compensation equal to the original purchase of an airline ticket.

May 25, 1995

Dr. Patricia McNeehan
Physicians & Surgeons Clinic
14332 Samaritan Way
Des Moines, Iowa 50612

Dear Dr. McNeehan

We were very concerned to learn of your experience on one of our flights. We agree that you should receive some compensation for bearing with the experience with such patience. The enclosed voucher entitles you to one free ticket to any of our destinations in the 48 contiguous states.

Your experience was far out of the ordinary, as you are probably aware. As one of our frequent-flier members, you have seen our dedicated crew members in action, working very hard to assure that all goes smoothly for our passengers, from the moment they book their flight until they reach their final destination, baggage in hand. You may be sure that we intend to continue our high level of commitment to your satisfaction.

Please accept our sincere apologies on behalf of Skyways Airlines. If I can be of further assistance, please call my direct line at 800-555-3121. We look forward to having you flying with us again soon.

Sincerely,

Wade Sutter
Customer Relations Manager

REPLACING DEFECTIVE EQUIPMENT

In this instance, the agreement to replace defective merchandise goes against company policy. Normally, customers would first have to send the product in for testing and repair. Note that the reply doesn't make a big deal of bending the rules, but does state what normal policy requires to avoid problems in the future. Also, the letter doesn't accept blame for the problem, nor does it imply blame on the part of the user. It simply acknowledges the problem and provides a solution. The specific cause of the defect will be sorted out and explained later. This letter is transmitted via fax because of the time crunch.

23 July 1995

Carmen Salinas, Operations Supervisor
Sasketech Industries
Box 2218
8843 Highway 153
Saskatoon, Saskatchewan S4T 4N2

Dear Carmen,

I was concerned to learn of the difficulty you encountered with the TS 111 robotics equipment. Normally, company policy requires that we test the equipment and repair it rather than replace it. However, because you are under such a tight deadline, I'll get a replacement to you overnight. We're glad to be able to help out. Fortunately, we have a replacement in stock.

Please arrange to have the defective equipment ready to exchange when our delivery truck arrives tomorrow afternoon. I appreciate your help with making this transfer. We will test the defective equipment to determine what the problem might be and let you know for future reference.

I wish you luck with your deadline. Please call me if I can be of further assistance.

Sincerely,

Thomas Bentworth
Industrial Support

CLARIFYING ACCOUNT BALANCE AND PAYMENT INFORMATION

[date]   RE: Account No.: [account#]

[name]
[address]
[city], [state] [zip

In response to your inquiry concerning International Orchardist Society publications, it is our pleasure to provide you with a review of the account.

You may wish to note that your remittance of [amount] was credited to the [product1] and not to the [product2]. Should your records not agree with ours, kindly return this letter with complete information. If you have made payments for which you have not been credited, please give the amount of the remittance and the cancellation date if a canceled check is available. Payments sent by money order or bank draft may be verified through the issuing office.

If any item listed has not been received, we can either arrange to forward a replacement or cancel the order, whichever you prefer. Material that you choose not to keep my be returned to our Walla Walla, Washington, headquarters with your name, address, and cancellation instructions attached.

When you write to us, you can be sure this concern will have our careful attention. We appreciate your interest in the Society and look forward to serving you in the future.

Sincerely yours,

Manager, Customer Service

ITEMS	DATE PAID	COST	SHIPPED	AMOUNT DUE
xxxx	xxxx	xxxx	xxxx	xxxx
xxxx	xxxx	xxxx	xxxx	xxxx
xxxx	xxxx	xxxx	xxxx	xxxx
xxxx	xxxx	xxxx	xxxx	xxxx

7 ■ APOLOGIZING FOR PROBLEMS/ERRORS

Customer service means sometimes having to say you're sorry. When the situation arises, you want to apologize gracefully without groveling, sincerely without placing blame on the customer. There are many times when apologies are appropriate, most especially when your company has made a mistake. Sometimes, though, an apology simply shows sympathy for the frustrations that the customer has experienced that are neither your fault nor the customer's. In those situations, saying "I'm sorry" is meant in the way saying "I'm sorry" to someone who has lost a loved one—you're sorry to hear that they're having difficulty.

In any case, it's important to maintain the company's dignity as well as a respectful attitude toward the customer. If explanations are needed, provide them succinctly. Most customers won't be interested in "excuses," but by briefly explaining the situation behind the problem you're apologizing for, you can sometimes win understanding.

APOLOGY FOR MISTAKE WITH SUBSCRIPTION

This letter is informing the customer know about a problem at the same time it apologizes. A routine survey of the company's books revealed a problem that the customer was probably not aware of. This will ultimately be a great goodwill vehicle—it lets customers know that their interests are being watched over even when they don't know it.

September 24, 1995

Karen Islington
P.O. Box 4321
Oklahoma City, OK 73102

Dear Ms. Islington:

During a recent investigation of our records we discovered that although we received instructions to change the address of your gift recipient to that shown below, mailing of the Quill Literary was discontinued in error. Please accept our apology for this oversight.

Delivery was stopped with the February 1995 issue. At that time the account was credited through December 1995. Normally, we would resume delivery and send the back issues. However, several magazines are now out of print.

Please verify whether or not the address shown below is correct for your recipient. Upon receipt of your reply, we will reinstate the account with the current issue and send you a confirmation of the new expiration date. A letter of apology will also be sent to your recipient.

Again, we apologize for the oversight. Your patience and courtesy in this matter is appreciated.

Sincerely yours,

Adam Marshall
Manager, Customer Service

E-MAIL APOLOGY FOR DELAYED RESPONSE TO REQUEST FOR RECEIPT

Note that the language is very informal, the salutation "Dear" is omitted, as is a closing such as "Sincerely." The "aka" at the bottom means that Rick's e-mail address name is SuperMedia, which in this case is the name of the company. The computer software that drives e-mail messages requires you to input the e-mail address of the sender and a subject line, which are included with the sender's e-mail address in a header. Often, because this information always appears at the top of the message, the greeting is left out altogether and the message begins with the first line of text. E-mail messages are almost always directed and signed with first names. Paragraphs are rarely more than two sentences long, and a space between paragraphs helps with readability.

Cheryl,

Sorry it took me so long to get back to you.

The orders have been coming in fast and furious and my first priority is always to make sure you get your products on time.

The written receipt you requested is on its way.

If you don't get it by Friday, or if you need me to fax a copy sooner, just e-mail me. I'll get right on it!

Thanks for your patience!

Rick
aka: SuperMedia

APOLOGIZING FOR OUT-OF-STOCK PRODUCTS

Customer service representatives often must deal with the fact that a customer's order just can't be filled. In this case, the products are only temporarily out of stock. It's a form letter that has also been personalized. Notice that although it has an individual name and address, the salutation is "Dear Agency Customer." This simplifies the question of having to add a courtesy title such as "Mr." or "Ms."

June 2, 1995

Clint McBrown
Assistant Director
ImPrint Services
P.O. Box 89C
Secaucus, NJ 07094

Dear Agency Customer,

We are sorry to inform you that the product(s) you ordered are temporarily out of stock. The item(s) on your order are listed below.

We have given your order highest priority, and as soon as the stock is replenished, your order will be on its way.

We again want to say we are sorry for the delay. Thank you for waiting.

Sincerely,

Agency Solutions
Customer Service Department
1-800-555-0221

Order #33321-33

Qty	Item	Description	Amount
1	B-221	Software bundle for CD-Rom	89.00
1	C-319	Promotional Package	12.95
1	C-311	Promotional Package for CD-Rom	12.95
		Subtotal	114.90
		Shipping	5.95
		Total	120.85

APOLOGIZING FOR DOUBLE CHARGE ON CREDIT CARD ACCOUNT

This is a serious error, one that you'll want to catch and correct before the customer receives a credit card invoice showing a double billing. This restaurant has just assured that J.R. and Susan Carmichael will become loyal customers—if they're not already. Catching your own mistakes and fessing up to them before the customer even knows about them demonstrates your honesty and reliability.

July 10, 1995

J.R. and Susan Carmichael
12 West Frontage Street
Albany, Oregon 97321

Dear Mr. and Mrs. Carmichael:

Thank you for your dining with us at Sam's Station on July 8.
It has come to our attention that, in error, your credit card account was charged twice.

Please be assured that a credit has been issued to your account, a copy of which is enclosed. The credit will appear on your next statement. We sincerely apologize for the error and any inconvenience you have been caused.

In appreciation for your understanding, please accept the enclosed signature discount card, which entitles you to a 25 percent discount any time you dine with us between now and October 31.

We appreciate your patronage and look forward to serving you again soon.

Sincerely,

Sam Alffenbluch
General Manager

APOLOGIZING FOR DELAYED RETURN

23 September, 1995

John and Alva Wilson
332 Patterson Drive
Manchester, TN 37355

Dear Mr. and Mrs. Wilson,

We received your comments concerning the delay in receiving your return premium check from the Tuassen Insurance Group and would like to thank you for the information you provided. It is always our goal to provide the best service to our policy holders.

I noted with concern the check issuance delay, and after an investigation found the following information for you. Our computer system calculates any policy return premium due and issues the applicable checks on a weekly basis through a file search program. An error occurred on your policy file during this search, and as a result of this error, the return premium check failed to generate promptly. The error has been corrected, and I enclose your check for the amount of $37.50.

Tuassen associates work hard to provide excellent service. Any delay in service is certainly unintentional and regrettable. Please accept my sincere apology for the inconvenience you have experienced.

Yours truly,

Pamela Fronmeyer
Manager, Client Support

APOLOGIZING FOR BILLING ERROR

November 5, 1995

D. J. Warren
1145 S. Main Street
Salt Lake City, UT 84106

Dear Mr. or Ms. Warren,

Thank you for your letter of October 7 which expressed your frustrations with some billing issues with your subscription. We apologize for the inconvenience and we do appreciate your being a subscriber to the Tribune.

Our records show that the $10 balance has been cleared. In addition, we have credited your account for another four weeks in the amount of $9.88.

Please accept this umbrella as a token of our appreciation for your newspaper subscription.

Once again, we apologize for the frustration and inconvenience you have experienced. If you have any more questions, please feel free to contact me personally at 555-1102.

Yours very truly,

Steve Fletcher
Circulation Administration Manager

APOLOGIZING FOR AN ERROR IN COMPANY ADVERTISING

One of the trickiest problems that can arise for customer service representatives is when a company advertisement presented incorrect information. Whether it was the company's fault or the newspaper's, it's essential to get the information corrected right away to avoid potential liability for false advertising. If you ran an ad that said all umbrellas in the store were $1.50 when in fact only a certain model was $1.50, you would be obliged to sell even that $50 Ralph Lauren umbrella for $1.50 if you didn't make an immediate effort to change the advertisement. Mistakes happen, but if you leave the mistake as it was, it starts to look as if you intended to lure customers in with promises you had no intention of fulfilling. Here's a form letter that apologizes for an incorrect advertised price and explains how the company corrected the mistake.

December 11, 1995

Dear Santina's Customer:

Thank you for your letter regarding our mid-December sale advertisement. We appreciate the time you took to let us know of the error, and we sincerely apologize for your disappointment at not finding the sale item at the price that was advertised by mistake in last Sunday's newspaper.

As can so easily happen, a number was transposed—from the correct price of $52.95 to $25.95—which made a big difference! We immediately called the newspaper, which ran a corrected ad on Tuesday. Unfortunately, that wasn't quickly enough to save several of our valued customers from a frustrating experience.

We want to thank you for your patience and understanding. We care about your business, and we want your trips to Santina's to be fulfilling. Therefore, please accept the enclosed 10% off coupon for your next visit.

Sincerely,

Joanna Rowlands
Customer Service Center

Apologizing for Referring Bill to Collection Agency in Error

May 11, 1995

Gina Stenopoulos
443 Akikana Drive
Honolulu, HI 88295

Dear Ms. Stenopoulos:

I am taking this opportunity to formally apologize to you for the mistake made on your account billing. Due to an error on our part, your gift subscription continued beyond the period ordered by the party giving you the gift. As a result, your account was placed for collection by mistake. We have cleared the outstanding balance on your account. Please accept our apology.

We have notified our collection agency and they have removed your name from their records. We have assured that there will be no negative effect on your credit rating.

Please accept the enclosed gift as a token of our sincere regret for the inconvenience we have caused you.

Thank you for making us aware of the mistake we made in your billing. Please let me know if there is anything else I can do to make this right. My direct phone number is 555-2211.

Sincerely,

Annette Lockridge
Customer Support Administrator

APOLOGIZING FOR DELAYED RESPONSE TO SUBSCRIPTION CANCELLATION

June 15, 1995

Ms. Joan Farris
221 West Sultana
Sandy, UT 84094

Dear Ms. Farris,

We apologize for the inconvenience you had to go through in canceling your subscription to the Salt Lake Tribune. I have checked your account and have verified that your subscription will be canceled as of the 17th of June. I have instructed our Accounting Department to issue you a refund of $9, which covers the period of April 4 through May 9. I have also instructed them to clear your account of any additional charges.

I again apologize for any inconvenience that our delay in stopping your subscription has caused. We hope to be able to serve you again soon. If you have any further problem with billing or delivery, please don't hesitate to call me personally at 555-1132.

Yours very truly,

Thomas Quentin
Circulation Marketing &
Customer Service Manager

APOLOGIZING FOR RUDENESS

Here's a letter from a customer service representative who—like many of us at one time or another—had just had too much to cope with one day and lost her cool. Rather than sit at her desk and cringe in remembrance every time she thought of the conversation with Mr. Sevilla, she wrote a sincere apology.

July 23, 1995

Ernesto Sevilla
334 Sampras Lane
Albuquerque, NM87121

Dear Mr. Sevilla:

I want to apologize for my abruptness with you in our telephone conversation yesterday. I'm afraid I didn't do a very good job of letting you know how important your call really was to me.

In my line of work, there can be no real excuses for treating customers with less than perfect courtesy. It had been about the worst day on record, but I should never have allowed my own problems or frustrations to have an effect on my dealings with important customers like you.

Please accept my apology. I look forward to talking with you in the future—and in some measure reaffirm our company's commitment to fast, *friendly* customer service.

With best regards,

Susan Morrisey
Customer Service Associate

Apologizing for Mistaken Collection Letters

September 13, 1995

Joseph Carlisle
P.O. Box 2231B
Granville, OH 43023

Dear Mr. Carlisle:

We apologize for the letters that you have received from Kingsfield Adjustment Bureau and Cross-State Collections.

I have personally spoken with the manager of our Collection Accounting division and have been assured that no further letters will be sent to you. Please be assured that at no time will any credit bureau receive any report of any type concerning your account.

We again apologize for any inconvenience that we have caused you. If you have any further questions or problems with your account, please contact me personally, collect, at (505) 555-3321.

Sincerely,

Julian Winnerly
Customer Service Manager

APOLOGIZING FOR MISINFORMATION

When you've given a customer some misinformation, it's important to clarify the mistake right away—before problems arise that could leave you holding the losing end of a lawsuit.

May 22, 1995

Horace Nieman
P.O. Box 4091
Detroit, MI 48211

Dear Mr. Nieman:

When you were in the office yesterday, we discussed the proposals for handling temporary staff on the construction site. I'm afraid I gave you some misinformation, and I want to clarify the matter so there's no confusion later on.

Garver Temporaries was not able to provide enough construction workers for the next six weeks. We've had to combine the available resources of three different temporary agencies. The end result is that we will have three separate payroll obligations instead of one, as we'd expected.

I apologize for giving you the wrong information. I hope this won't affect your plans. If you need me to make any changes in the contracts, please call me and I'll see to everything.

Thank you for your understanding.

Sincerely,

Joshua Hokusai
Operations Supervisor

8 ■ RESPONDING TO CUSTOMER COMPLAINTS

It's impossible to anticipate every kind of customer complaint. The possibilities vary from industry to industry. The examples below, therefore, attempt to present the various attitudes that you can take as the customer service representative, and some of the range of expressions that can help you maintain a good relationship with your customers in light of their complaints.

EXPRESSING APPRECIATION FOR CUSTOMER COMPLAINT

One of the best ways to disarm a complaint is to thank the customer for making it. By showing your genuine appreciation for their taking the time to let you know about the problem, you impress your customers with your caring and your commitment. You may not be acceding to all their demands, but you communicate your willingness to listen and to respond with fairness. This is a personalized form letter that allows the customer service representative to provide the missing information about whether the customer telephoned or wrote a letter, what product was not satisfactory, and the appropriate contact person to be called for more information.

[LETTER DATE]

[CUSTOMER NAME/ADDR]
[ADDRESS LINE 1]
[ADDRESS LINE 2]
[CITY, STATE ZIP]

Dear [SALUTATION]:

Thank you for taking the time to [METHOD DESC] us about [PRODUCT/DESC1]. We are sorry your purchase was not satisfactory. Please accept the enclosed check to reimburse you for the costs you incurred.

Meanwhile, we have informed our Operations Services Department of the situation. They will investigate and, if necessary, take appropriate corrective measures to be sure that our products will always meet the very highest standards.

Coors Brewing Company is committed to providing consumers with the best-quality product possible. Your feedback helps us maintain that quality, and we appreciate your taking the time to contact us.

If you have further questions, please call the [PRODUCT CONTACT].

[USER CLOSING]

[USER NAME]
[USER TITLE]
[USER DEPARTMENT]

[USER INITIALS] [REF NUMBER]
[CARBON COPIES]

[ENCLOSURES]

RESPONDING TO COMPLAINT ABOUT PRODUCT SHELF LIFE

Although this letter might hint at some responsibility on the part of the customer, it clearly focuses on the desire to inform so that future problems can be avoided. The message of thanks and the compensation—the issue the customer is most interested in—are in the very first paragraph.

July 18, 1995

Thomas C. Norton
Director of Laboratory Supply
Maddix Medical Center
1212 W. Harborside
Providence, RI 02919

Dear Mr. Norton:

Thank you for your letter about the chemical reagent that lost effectiveness after one year. Please accept the enclosed credit voucher, which may be used for replacement chemicals or returned for a cash refund.

J.J. Chemicals is striving continually to prepare stable formulations and to devise ways of packaging them to provide the maximum protection.

Most chemicals and prepared reagents do not, by themselves, deteriorate after their manufacture. Storage conditions and packaging have a definite influence on chemical stability. Reagents should be stored in a cool, dry place for maximum life. It is a good practice to date chemicals upon receipt and rotate your supplies. The absorption of moisture, carbon dioxide and/or other gases from the atmosphere, bacterial action, or light in the case of photosensitive compounds may have an affect on the life of a chemical reagent. In some cases, reaction with the storage container itself, or interaction of several ingredients may occur.

In reference to your question, our dating code system works as follows:

Unless otherwise indicated, our reagents have an indefinite shelf life, which should be confirmed against fresh standards at one year's time and at regular intervals after that. These products would be designated with an alpha and numeric lot code, such as 14AG. Any products for which special storage conditions are recommended have this noted on their labels.

There are a few J.J. Chemical reagents that have finite shelf life. These chemical reagents are designated with a four-digit lot code, such as 5043. The first digit designates the year in which the product was made. The last three digits designate the day of the year that the material was made. The above lot number, for example, indicates that the product was made on the 43rd day of 1995, or February 12. These products should be checked regularly against a known standard to confirm their continued performance. Proper storage conditions will extend the shelf life.

Thank you for your interest in J.J. Chemical products. Should you have any questions, please call our Customer Service Department at 800-555-2152.

Sincerely,

Roanna McDowell
Customer Service Associate

REPLYING TO CUSTOMER WHO MISUNDERSTOOD DELIVERY TIME

Any letter that has to tell the customer he or she was wrong—no matter how subtly—needs to include a message of thanks. You might thank a customer for his order, for her previous loyalty, or for taking the time to write with a concern. The letter below shows appreciation as well as sympathy, even though the message is clear that the company was not at fault. At no time, though, does the letter blame the customer or even say directly that she misunderstood the situation. The explanation that delivery time is noted on the order form is the only suggestion that the information had been available to the customer if she'd read it.

February 2, 1995

Ms. Serita Davis
2231 South Lawn Ave.
Boulder, CO 80303

Dear Ms. Davis:

I appreciate your letter explaining your frustration at missing the Federal Express delivery of your order. I want to thank you for taking the time to write.

When you requested second-day delivery by Federal Express, you were automatically scheduled to receive your package no later than noon on January 29. Only priority next-day air packages are guaranteed to arrive by 10 a.m., which is noted in the customer service guidelines on our order form.

For future reference, you can arrange to have the package left by signing a release form with Federal Express. That way you won't be required to miss work to wait for delivery. You can also specify that packages be delivered to your work address, if that would be more convenient.

Be assured that we are ready to work with you to make sure you get the service you want. Again, thank you for writing. If I can be of any further help, please call me at (303) 555-2298.

Sincerely yours,

Tamara Gardner
Assistant Manager

PROVIDING INFORMATION ABOUT POLICY AND INSTRUCTIONS FOR RETURNING UN-WANTED MERCHANDISE

Here is another form letter that the customer service representative calls up and replaces the "xxxx" entries with the specific information. Any character could be used to mark places that need to be filled in individually, but "xx" is a good one because the two letters aren't together in any words that would be missed in a computer spell check. (Using the spell check feature in your word processor is always a good idea just before you're ready to print—one of the great benefits of word processing over typewriters!)

xxxx xx, 19xx

xxxx
xxxx
xxxx

Dear xxxx:

Thank you for responding to our notice for the Quill Literary Society's xxxx.

We take this opportunity to assure you that the Society maintains a strict policy whereby we never forward unsolicited material. As the result of your instructions on a previous order, your name was placed on our permanent mailing list to receive our new xxxx upon release. This material may be examined and either kept or returned.

If you do not wish to keep the material you have received, you need only return it with your request for cancellation.

Any inconvenience this may have caused is sincerely regretted. We look forward to your continued affiliation with the Quill Literary Society.

Sincerely yours,

Manager, Customer Service

Enclosure

RESPONDING TO DELIVERY PROBLEM COMPLAINT

Notice that this letter delves right into the message of thanks and follows with a proactive statement that this company wants to find solutions.

December 14, 1995

Ms. Donna Halvorson
1124 West Lafayette
Terre Haute, IN 46201

Dear Ms. Halvorson:

Thank you for your telephone call today. We appreciate your giving us a chance to look into the problem of late delivery and find some solutions.

My investigation of the late delivery in your area revealed several factors that contributed to the problem over the last week or two, including weather conditions and shortage of delivery personnel. We are doing all in our power to rectify these situations so that you can once again enjoy on-time delivery.

Once again, we appreciate the opportunity to serve you and pledge to continue to work on correcting this problem. As a token of our appreciation for your continued support, please accept this gift. If you have any further problems, feel free to call me at 555-1123.

Yours very truly,

Robert Farris
Customer Service Manager

RF:cl
Enc.
cc: John Howe, Distribution Manager

EXPLAINING POSSIBLE CAUSES FOR EQUIPMENT MALFUNCTION

Expressing your concern about problems your customer is having with your products or services is one way to avoid either accepting or placing blame. In the situation below, the engineering department told the customer service manager that the problem was caused by the atmospheric conditions at the customer's plant, but this letter takes an indirect approach. The letter offers assurances and various options for taking care of the problem.

26 March 1995

Mr. Ronald Sheldrake
Caravan Manufacturers, Inc.
Box 2319
Bismarck, ND 58501

Dear Mr. Sheldrake:

I was concerned to learn of the problems you have experienced with the high-speed drill assembly unit we installed for you in 1993. I am pleased to know the problems involve its appearance rather than its performance.

I have consulted with our engineering department about the corrosion of the casing. John Brye, our chief technical specialist, assures me that although it may look unsightly, the casing is the stopgap against corrosion of the more important inner mechanisms.

To correct the visual appearance, John suggests applying a coating of a rust-resistant paint, then a plastic resin-type coating. We could perform this for you in our factory, but you would lose valuable production time. John has readied the necessary materials and instructions for immediate shipment to your plant, if you'd prefer to handle it yourself. Just let me know what you decide.

The corrosion itself may be caused by severe temperature changes combined with high humidity. If you apply salt to your parking areas during freezing weather, some of the salinity may transfer to the air and worsen the reactions.

I look forward to hearing from you. As always, we're committed to giving you the best products along with the best service. Our support doesn't stop with the bill of sale.

Sincerely,

James Robinson
Manager, Customer Support

RESPONDING TO AN UNJUSTIFIED COMPLAINT

Many times, the problems you deal with come about because of a mistake the customer made, but the customer feels it was your fault in some way. Here's a letter that tactfully explains the customer's and printer's responsibilities without assigning—or wrongly accepting—blame.

January 12, 1995

Ms. Patricia Kingsford
Advertising Manager
Hartsfield Insurance Co.
2231 West Parkway
Dayton, Ohio 45412

Dear Ms. Kingsford:

We were concerned to receive your letter expressing your disappointment with the brochure we printed for you last week. It's all too common to find a typographical error only when it's in final printed form— no matter how many people have proofread it!

We sympathize with your frustration because we've experienced it with our own printed pieces. While we take every effort to produce flawless publications for our customers, we must rely on you to be the final approval.

The process of putting together a printed piece involves a great many steps and many people. Our part of that process requires us to prepare film from the mechanicals your artist provides; create proofs from the film for your final approval; make any changes that you specify after carefully proofreading the final proofs, making additional proofs if you require them; and printing the job to your specifications.

When artwork is created by another party and not in our plant, we do not proofread the content; we check only for problems that might occur in printing, such as misplaced margins or improper crop marks.

The proof copy that you sign, approving the job for printing, emphasizes the need for careful proofreading for just this kind of situation. The only solution, at this stage, is to reprint if you feel the typographical error is too serious to let stand.

If you reprint, the cost will be reduced by about 27 percent because you have already incurred the basic set-up costs for film and plates. Please call me if you would like a precise quote on reprinting costs.

Thank you for your understanding. I look forward to hearing from you.

Sincerely,

John Rettig
Customer Service

9 ■ RESPONDING TO CUSTOMER PRAISE

The opportunity to write these letters doesn't come along nearly often enough, but this is one opportunity you never want to pass up. If a customer has taken the time to give you a pat on the back, it's essential to acknowledge that effort with a reply. Here are a few examples.

THANKING CUSTOMER FOR COMMENTS AND PROVIDING INFORMATION

When a customer writes to report success with your products or services, always take the time to say thank you. But then you might go the extra mile, as the writer below does in response to a letter about gardening supplies.

15 September 1995

Mr. Quentin Farmer
883 Grass Hollow Lane
Abbotsford, British Columbia V6H 1C3
CANADA

Dear Mr. Farmer:

Thank you for taking the time to write about your pleasure in the *Growstarter* compound. We are always delighted to hear success stories such as yours, and we're particularly impressed with the results you've accomplished—85 pounds of tomatoes from one plant in a single day! That may be one for the record books!

You mentioned that you had less success with your harvest of green peppers. I checked with our resident botanist, Helen Channing, and she recommends that for your location and climate, you could add a pH neutralizer to the soil about a month before planting. Once sprouts appear, apply the *Growstarter* weekly instead of twice monthly for the first month, then follow the standard instructions.

I wish you luck with next year's harvest! And thank you again for writing. Your comments really mean a lot to us.

Yours sincerely,

Donald McFarland
Customer Service Department

SAYING THANKS FOR CUSTOMER COMPLIMENT

If you're in the enviable position of having several complementary letters to reply to, you might set up a form letter like the one below. I wouldn't send a form letter in response to a customer compliment unless, like this one, it was set up to be personalized.

[LETTER DATE]

[CUSTOMER NAME/ADDR]
[ADDRESS LINE 1]
[ADDRESS LINE 2]
[CITY, STATE ZIP]

Dear [SALUTATION]:

Thank you for taking the time to [METHOD DESC] us about [PRODUCT DESC1]. We appreciate your letting us know how much you enjoy it.

We always like hearing from our customers. We go to great lengths to assure all our products meet the highest standards of quality, and it is especially gratifying to hear from a satisfied customer.

Again, thank you for your courtesy in letting us know how you feel. We hope you'll continue to enjoy our products.

[USER CLOSING]

[USER NAME]
[USER TITLE]
[USER DEPARTMENT]

[USER INITIALS]
[REF NUMBER]
[CARBON COPIES]

[ENCLOSURES]

THANKING CUSTOMER FOR LETTER PRAISING EMPLOYEES

When customers praise your employees, you want to respond personally with a very appreciative note of thanks. You'll also want to share the letter with others in your operation—nothing motivates employees like seeing someone else praised for a job well done.

March 25, 1995

Janet Ikida
334 W. Marshall
Bennington, 05201

Dear Ms. Ikida:

Thank you so much for your wonderful letter! It's comments like yours that remind us why we at Grace Brothers enjoy coming to work. Though it may sound strange, we've sometimes had to work hard to keep up the sense of fun and enjoyment you experienced. We want both our employees and our customers to think of being at Grace Brothers as one of the day's highlights.

Thank you for taking the time to let us know how we're doing. We really appreciate hearing from you and hope you'll continue to let us make shopping "lighthearted"!

With warmest regards,

Celia La Conner
Support Services

10 ■ PROCESSING ORDERS AND PAYMENTS

Many large companies have separate departments to handle order processing, but frequently dealing with any irregularities in orders or payments falls to the customer service department. Here are several examples for common situations in handling orders and payments.

APPRECIATION FOR ORDER, WITH DELIVERY INFORMATION

Any letter regarding an order should begin—and probably end—with a note of appreciation for the customer's business. This letter provides information about delivery dates and lets the customer know his responsibilities for making sure the order proceeds smoothly.

August 15, 1995

Mr. Ivan Washburn
Veterans Affairs Medical Center
11222 South Haven Boulevard
Santa Monica, CA 91123

RE: Your Order #221148

Dear Mr. Washburn:

On behalf of the Premier Medical Products Company, I would like to thank you for your order.

Please note that your purchase order number 221148 covering hospital beds and accessories has been entered on Premier Sales Order numbers 3531, 3532, 3533, and 3534. I understand that you are requesting staggered delivery beginning September 15 and continuing monthly through January of next year. Your architects must submit drawings and plans for the mounted accessories prior to September 1 to assure timely delivery. As soon as all manufacturing details have been finalized, I will send a formal acknowledgment confirming shipping dates.

Should you have any questions or need additional information, please contact Mr. Smith, our accessories manufacturing coordinator, or myself at any time.

Thank you again for selecting Premier to supply your hospital's needs.

Sincerely yours,

June Novielle
Customer Service Administrator
Architectural Products Division

FINAL CONFIRMATION OF ORDER AND SHIPPING DATES

This letter provides a follow-up to the one above. It confirms the details and again expresses the company's appreciation for the order.

September 8, 1995

Mr. Ivan Washburn
Veterans Affairs Medical Center
11222 South Haven Boulevard
Santa Monica, CA 91123

RE: Your Order #221148

Dear Mr. Washburn:

On behalf of the Premier Medical Products Company, I am pleased to inform you that all manufacturing details on your purchase order number 221148 have been finalized.

As the enclosed acknowledgment copies of Premier Sales Order numbers 3531, 3532, 3533, and 3534 indicate, the first part of your order is scheduled to load on a truck the week of September 15. As soon as more specific delivery information becomes available, Ms. Dawson of our shipping division will contact you personally. Each subsequent shipment will follow the first at 30-day intervals, as you requested.

Meanwhile, should you have any questions or need additional information, please contact Ms. Dawson or myself at any time.

Once again, thank you again for this very nice order.

Sincerely yours,

June Novielle
Customer Service Administrator
Architectural Products Division

REQUESTING ADDITIONAL INFORMATION TO PROCESS ORDER

One of the most common problems in order processing is missing information. This form letter deals with frequently requested information in a direct, clear manner.

Dear Pimlico Customer:

Thank you for your purchase order dated _____ . Unfortunately, we are unable to process the order without the following information:

1. Current catalog numbers (catalog enclosed)
2. Telephone number and contact person's name
3. Physical address for UPS delivery
4. Address for billing
5. Price approval for items being ordered

If you have questions or need assistance, please contact Customer Service at 800-555-2277. Thank you for supplying the necessary information. We will process your order immediately upon receipt.

Sincerely,

Customer Service Department

RESPONDING TO QUERY ABOUT ORDER: NO RECORD OF ORDER RECEIVED

February 11, 1995

Patricia Neeland
Branch Manager
County Bank
P.O. Box 2219
New Orleans, LA 70812

Dear Ms. Neeland:

Thank you for your recent letter asking about the status of your order.

However, we have no record of your Zenon hardware order. We have tried to contact you by telephone but have been unable to reach you personally. We're sending this letter with instructions for placing your order.

We will expedite shipment as soon as we receive your order. We will also ship your product via overnight delivery at our expense. Orders must be prepaid; we accept checks (U.S. dollars and drawn on a U.S. bank), Visa, MasterCard, American Express, or domestic purchase orders (originals only).

Thank you for your interest in our products. If you have any questions or need further assistance, please contact our office at 800-555-1231 or by fax at 504-555-1243. My e-mail address is dbsmith@zenon.com

Sincerely,

Daniel B. Carlisle
Customer Service

RETURNING AN ORDER; SPECIAL OFFER EXPIRED

Mail order companies have a special problem to deal with: catalogs that have been buried on the customer's desk so long that the prices have changed or products have become obsolete or unavailable before the order is ever placed. In the situation below, the company chose to return the order rather try to substitute other products for those no longer available.

March 30, 1995

Guadalupe Martinez
Interstate Commercial Services
56 West Viejo
Phoenix, Arizona 85023

Dear Ms. Martinez:

Thank you for your recent order for the Zenon Systems 5000 computer system and bundled software/CD Rom drive.

Unfortunately, we are unable to process your request as it stands because the special offer expired more than two months ago and some of the software offered is no longer available. I have enclosed our most recent catalog, which includes other offers that might be of interest.

Please accept our apologies for any inconvenience this may cause. We appreciate your understanding and your continued interest in Zenon Systems products. Please call if I can answer any questions about our current special offers.

Sincerely,

Susan Chen
Manager, Customer Service Department

PROVIDING SHIPPING INFORMATION AND PRICES

This routine form letter thanks customers for their orders and provides information on shipping charges. It is not intended to go out with every order but only to those customers who requested the shipping information.

Dear Pimlico Customer:

We wish to thank you for your purchase order and advise you that our terms are F.O.B. Shipping Point (Tucson, Arizona). Shipping charges will be prepaid and added to the invoice as a separate line item.

Pimlico has simplified freight charges for all U.S. orders with a U.S. shipping destination. Orders totaling up to $24.99 will be charged $5.00 for shipping; $25.00–$49.99 will be $7; $50.00–$199.99 will be $9.00; $200.00–$499.99 will be $12; and orders over $500.00 will be $15.00. Priority shipments via second day and next day delivery are available. Please contact our Customer Service Department at 800-555-1124 for more information.

Pimlico's credit terms are net 30 days.

Thank you for choosing Pimlico products. We appreciate the opportunity to serve you.

Sincerely,

Charles Moregood
V.P. Customer Service

NOTIFYING CUSTOMERS OF LATE DELIVERY

Most manufacturers have had this problem at least once: You've developed sent a product, announced it in the media with a release date, only to have problems in production that keep you from meeting your deadline. Meanwhile, eager customers have sent in their orders and are calling daily to find out when they can expect your exciting new product. Here's a form letter that was personalized for each customer who had ordered.

June 23, 1995

[firstname] [lastname]
[title]
[company]
[address1]
[address2]
[city], [state] [zip]

Dear [salutation] [lastname]:

Thank you for your order for our new product, the DMG-K1000. We are very excited about its development and know you are eager to receive your order.

Because we want to make sure that the DMG-K1000 is fully tested to assure the highest possible quality, we have delayed the final production date for [timedelay]. Our commitment to quality sometimes demands that we bite the bullet and make the tough decisions. In the end, though, we know that it's our reputation for providing our customers with the best in diagnostic technology that keeps you coming back to us year after year.

We will inform you immediately of any further changes to this scheduled release date. If you have any questions or concerns, please call me directly at 206/555-0221, ext. 223.

Sincerely yours,

Rod Waldren
Services and Support

FOLLOW-UP LETTER INQUIRING ABOUT DELAYED ORDER APPROVAL

This letter is both asking the customer for a response and providing a warning that prices are going to change if he doesn't respond soon. The tone is fairly formal and firm because of the need to convey that the matter is serious. Even so, the letter includes an expression of concern and a note of thanks.

July 1, 1995

Barker Industrial Associates
One S.W. Columbia
Portland, OR 97022

Attn: Milosh Feinberg

Dear Mr. Feinberg:

Your purchase order #228457 was received at Belle Terre Manufacturing on January 3, 1995. At that time we sent you an engineering specifications sheet with a request for final engineering approval prior to manufacturing and production. The letter stated that we would hold the request for six months.

We are concerned that we have not heard from you. We may not be able to continue to hold pricing. Please let us know if we need to prepare an updated quote for you. If we have placed this order for you under an updated purchase order, please disregard this notice.

If I can be of assistance, please call me on my direct line at 1-800-555-2221. We want to thank you for your order and your continued interest in Belle Terre Manufacturing.

Sincerely yours,

Kelly West
Customer Service Associate
Order Management Group

THANKING CUSTOMER FOR PAYMENT AND PROVIDING INFORMATION

Dear Subscriber,

Thank you for your recent payment for the *Idleyld Journal of Management*. If you are a new subscriber, you will receive your first issue soon. If you are renewing your subscription, you will enjoy uninterrupted service.

Whether you're new to *Idleyld* or a long-time reader, I know you will encounter a range of new, challenging ideas and thought-provoking insights into the world of management.

Free access to our on-line bulletin board is one of the benefits of your subscription. If you have a computer and a modem, you can make connections with managers from all over the country, in all areas of business and industry. Each bulletin board subject area has a guest host who helps subscribers find answers to their questions. I've enclosed an access guide that provides complete instructions for joining the ongoing bulletin board discussions.

Thank you again for your payment. If you have any questions regarding your subscription or our on-line service, please call me at (390) 555-2011 or e-mail me at customer.service@idleyld.org.

Sincerely,

Paula Hazlett
On-Line Support Manager
Customer Service Department

INFORMING CUSTOMER THAT PRODUCT IS NOT AVAILABLE

January 16, 1995

Joyce Mettler
Office Manager
Pyramid Systems, Inc.
455 Main Street, Suite 432
Seattle, WA 98110

Dear Ms. Mettler:

Thank you for your recent order.

Unfortunately, Brabant Electronics does not offer the product you are requesting and therefore we are returning the order to you. I have enclosed a new catalog of our products. If you would like to resubmit your order for a similar product, please make the changes and resend your order to Order Administration.

You can also retrieve a Brabant Electronics product list and information through our automated facsimile retrieval system by calling 800-555-4311. Select Document #100 for a complete index of available documents. You will receive the information by fax within a few minutes of making your call.

If you should have further questions or need additional assistance, please contact Brabant directly at 800-555-1123 or 206-555-0118.

We apologize for any inconvenience this may cause and appreciate your support of Brabant Electronics.

Sincerely,

Order Administration Department

INFORMING CUSTOMER OF SOON-TO-EXPIRE PURCHASE ORDER

March 14, 1995

Marion County Public Health Department
Building Three
County Services Complex
Marion, ND 58423

Attention: Purchasing

We would like to take this opportunity to inform you that your blanket purchase order number 445229 will expire shortly.

We have enclosed an updated quote with current pricing. If you wish to renew this blanket, please send your new order to my attention. We would like to be certain there will be no delay in fulfilling your future orders.

If I can be of further assistance, please call me at 1-800-555-2131. Thank you for your continued support of ChemField products.

Sincerely,

Dierdre Howe
Customer Service Representative

11 ■ CANCELING ORDERS/SERVICES

When the customer wants to sever your relationship, you need to accept that decision gracefully. That doesn't mean you can't express your desire that the customer will return. The letters below provide confirmation to customers who have requested that their subscriptions, memberships, or services be terminated, but each with a different approach.

RESPONDING TO A REQUEST TO CANCEL SERVICE

This cancellation letter accepts the customer's decision without question but adds that there may be a final invoice for outstanding charges. Note that at the end the writer expresses the hope that the company will be of service in the future.

> Dear Cellular One Customer,
>
> This is to confirm that we have received your 30-day written request to cancel your Cellular Once service. Cellular telephone number [phone no.] for account number [acct no.] was terminated as of [term. date].
>
> You will be billed for any long distance or roaming charges as we receive tapes on them. You could receive a bill up to 60 to 90 days from now reflecting these charges. All current charges will be billed to you on the statement that you will receive approximately _____. The amount currently owed as of today is $ _____ .
>
> If we can do anything else, let us know. We hope that we can be of service in the future.
>
> Sincerely,
>
> Client Service Representative

CANCELING SUBSCRIPTION AND REQUESTING VERIFICATION OF INSTRUCTIONS

This letter, too, accepts the customer's decision to cancel but needs to ask the customer how to deal with a credit balance. The letter ends with an assurance of prompt action and an expression of thanks for the customer's interest.

[date]

[firstname] [lastname]
[address]
[city], [state] [zip]

Dear [firstname] [lastname]:

We received your request to discontinue delivery of the *Xpressions* magazine. Your account is credited through [expiration].

Please verify your exact instructions below regarding the credit which remains on your account. Return this entire letter in the envelope provided. Your response will receive our careful and prompt attention.

Thank you for considering *Xpressions*.

Sincerely,

Customer Service Manager

Please indicate your instructions for the credit balance:

☐ Continue to provide delivery through the expiration date

☐ Discontinue delivery immediately and refund any remaining credit

☐ Discontinue delivery immediately and transfer remaining credit to provide delivery to the person listed below:

☐ Transfer to: _____

_____

NOTIFYING SUBSCRIBER OF DELIVERY CANCELLATION

Rather than simply suggest that someday the customer might want to subscribe again, this letter provides specific information about how to renew a canceled subscription.

March 15, 1995

Joel Stuber
15153 S. Peoria Road
Pershing, IL 61021

Dear Mr. Stuber:

This letter is to confirm that your Sunday-only subscription to the *Deseret News* has been canceled and your payment was credited to your account. As of the above date, your account (No. D33299) shows a zero balance.

We appreciate the opportunity that we had to deliver the *Deseret News* to you, and we are sorry that you have decided not to subscribe at the present time. If you decide to once again invite the *Deseret News* into your home, please call me, toll free, at 1-800-555-0012, extension 3322. We hope to hear from you again soon.

Yours sincerely,

Gunnar Sorensen
Circulation Administration Manager

CANCELING MEMBERSHIP AND NOTIFYING OF CREDIT BALANCE

Many mail order companies, book clubs, gardening clubs, and others involve membership programs. Inevitably, customers will want to cancel their memberships. The best way to deal with these requests is with a gracious acceptance, as well as an offer to be there when they're ready to renew. In this case, the member has a credit balance, and the gardening book club suggests that rather than cash the check, the member may choose to select a final book. I received this letter—and bought the book rather than cash the $9.35 check. In fact, I bought a $25 book, so the book club ended up getting more from this simple suggestion than saving the cash. This is a form letter that could easily be incorporated into a computer program to allow for personalization.

Dear Member:

We've canceled your book club membership as you requested. In doing so, we've noticed you have a credit balance, and have enclosed a check for that amount.

Before receiving your cancellation request, we mailed your last club bulletin. Why don't you use this check to buy one more book at the low member price? You can simply sign the enclosed refund check and mail it back to us along with your order. The amount of the check will be credited to your account. If the purchase price is larger than the amount of your refund check, we'll bill you later for the difference.

Buying a book from this last club bulletin in no way obligates you to stay in the club. Your membership has already been canceled, but we will gladly honor your refund check.

We've enjoyed having you as a member of our book club, and we're looking forward to the time when you may decide to join us again.

Sincerely,

Carrie Adams
Customer Service

12 ■ Responding to Credit/Payment Problems or Questions

So many things can go wrong between the time an order is placed and sent and the payment received and processed that it's impossible to provide examples for every situation here. The examples below are among the most common situations. The key word is courtesy, and there are three basic elements: thanking the customer for the order or the payment, explaining the problem in nonjudgmental language, and prescribing a clear action that can resolve the issue.

Informing Patron That Postdated Checks Cannot Be Accepted

18 June 1995

Bryce Ellison
Box 2245, Star Route 2
Bismarck, ND 55332

Dear Mr. Ellison:

Thank you for your check in payment of our invoice No. 22231. We note that you have chosen to postdate this payment.

In the past, we have accommodated this practice, but due to fees charged by banking institutions for processing this kind of payment, we will no longer be able to honor postdated checks.

We will, in this instance, apply your payment on the requested date. However, in future, your checks must be mailed to us with a current, cashable date.

The savings realized by our new procedure will insure our ability to maintain the lowest possible costs for our customers. We appreciate your cooperation.

Best regards,

Warren Sullivan
Customer Relations Associate

FORM LETTER FOR RESPONDING TO SHIPPING OR BILLING QUESTIONS

This letter addresses the most common problems that this company encounters. The customer service representative checks the appropriate box or boxes and fills in missing information. The customer can quickly scan to see what is required and provide the necessary response.

Thank you for your recent inquiry. We are happy to assist you in any way we can. Please find the information you are requesting below.

[ ] We contacted Federal Express at 1-800-238-5355 to track this order. This package was delivered on _____ / _____ / _____ at ___:___ am/pm, and signed for by _____.

[ ] After a careful search of our records, we are unable to locate a return. Please have the card-member provide proof of delivery or contact our Customer Service office at 1-800-555-0212.

[ ] This product was purchased under a delayed billing option. Both the order and the billing section have been included for your convenience.

[ ] This product is for an Anti-Virus Subscription Service that ships on an irregular basis. If you have not received your update yet, please be assured it will be sent to you during our next shipment, scheduled for _____.

[ ] This charge is for a Technical Support phone call. Please find enclosed a copy of the call overview.

[ ] _____

_____

Thank you for your patience and understanding in this matter. We apologize for any inconvenience this may have caused. Should you wish to reach us by phone, our Customer Service number is 1-800-555-0212.

LETTER EXPLAINING THAT CUSTOMER PAYMENT WAS INCOMPLETE

Rather than cash the customer's first check and invoice for the balance, this company returns the check for the customer to send the correct amount. Notice that an attempt was made to reach the customer by telephone first.

February 16, 1995

Karyn Jenkins
Carmine Enterprises
P.O. Box 54-9
Santa Fe, NM 87502

Dear Ms. Jenkins:

Thank you for your order. Unfortunately, the payment amount included doesn't completely cover the cost of the order. Please include payment for the amount of the product, shipping and handling ($10 for the first package and $5 for each additional package) and the appropriate sales tax amount for your state.

We have tried to contact you by telephone and have been unable to reach you. If you would like to resubmit your order, please include the enclosed order form with the corrected amount and we will promptly fill your order.

Please include a street address and the disk size you prefer, if this applies to your order. If you have any questions regarding the pricing of your order, or need additional assistance, please contact our Customer Service line at 800-555-0112.

Thank you for your continued support of our products.

Sincerely,

Juliana Davison
Customer Service

RETURNING CHECK FOR SIGNATURE

March 12, 1995

James D. Fremont
Parker Enterprises Ltd.
Suite 211
Farmington Building
Farmington, CT 06032

Dear Mr. Fremont:

Thank you for your recent order. However, because all orders must be prepaid, we are unable to process your order because the accompanying check was not signed.

We have your order packaged and ready to ship, awaiting your return of the enclosed check with your signature.

If you have any questions or need additional assistance, please contact me directly at 800-555-1192, or by fax at 550-555-2911.

Thank you for helping us serve you promptly.

Sincerely,

David Rawson
Customer Service Associate

EXPLAINING THAT CREDIT CARD WAS NOT ACCEPTED

When a customer's credit card is not approved, the letter explaining the problem needs to carefully avoid any hint that the customer is at fault. The letter below deftly skirts the question of exceeded credit limits by suggesting that the number might have been recorded incorrectly and asking the customer for verification.

todaydate

name *lastname*
company
address
city, *state* *zip*

Dear *title* *lastname*:

Thank you for your recent order.

Unfortunately, during our bank transmission, your credit card number was not accepted. We have tried to reach you by telephone and have been unable to contact you personally. Please verify the number and expiration date in case we processed your number incorrectly. According to our records, your number is:

CC#   *Exp. Date*

In order to expedite your request, please call Customer Service at (800) 555-3210 to provide the correct number. You may also mail your order and payment directly to our order processing department at the address below.

If you have any further questions or need additional assistance, please contact us directly or fax to (716) 555-2094.

Sincerely,

Customer Service

CS/fld

REQUESTING DIFFERENT CREDIT CARD OR PAYMENT METHOD

November 3, 1995

Torval Jorgensen
3322 West Michigan Avenue
Anchorage, Alaska 99540

Dear Mr. Jorgensen:

Thank you for your recent order for Zenon products.

Unfortunately, we are unable to process your order on the Discover card. We are able to accept orders on Visa, MasterCard, or American Express. We have tried to reach you by telephone but have been unable to contact you personally.

In order to expedite your order, please call Customer Service at (800) 555-4319 or Prepaid Order Processing at (800) 555-1238, and place your order on one of the above credit cards. Mention order number 65-9938 to further simplify the process. We have kept your order on record and can ship as soon as we receive your payment information.

You may also choose to send payment by mail (check or money order in U.S. funds) to our Prepaid Order Processing Department at the address below.

If you have any questions or need further assistance, please call the Customer Service department directly.

Thank you for your understanding and your continued interest in Zenon.

Sincerely,

Customer Service Department

REQUESTING NEW PAYMENT; CREDIT CARD NOT APPROVED

todaydate

name *lastname*
company
address
city, *state* *zip*

Dear *title* *lastname*:

We appreciate your order, dated June 15. On June 21 we sent a letter notifying you that our bank did not approve your credit card. We are writing again to let you know that we still show your order as pending.

The credit card number we have on file for you is *CC#*, Expiration *Exp Date*. The price of the *Product* is *Price*; the shipping and handling charge is *S&H Charge*; tax is *tax*. Your total is *Total*.

If the above payment information is not correct, please make the necessary changes when resubmitting your order. We will accept payment by check or money order, or by Visa, American Express, or MasterCard. If you are responding by mail, please include this letter with your payment. You may also call us directly at 800-555-3211. Please mention this letter when you call.

If we have not heard from you within 30 days, we will assume you no longer want this product and your order will be canceled.

Sincerely,

Customer Service

RETURNING ORDER FOR PAYMENT IN U.S. FUNDS

Notice here that rather than try to guess—and inevitably guess wrongly—whether "J.K." is a Mr. or a Ms., this letter writer repeats the initials in the salutation.

August 22, 1995

J.K. Gorman
P. O. Box 44231
Amarillo, TX 79112

Dear J.K. Gorman:

Thank you for your recent order. Unfortunately, we cannot process your order because all checks must be made payable in U.S. dollars and drawn on a U.S. bank. For your convenience, we accept American Express, MasterCard, and Visa.

When making your payment, please be sure to include your local sales tax and shipping and handling charges. Shipping and handling charges are $10 for the first product and $5 for each additional product.

If you have any further questions, or if you need additional assistance, please contact Zenon directly at (800) 555-1293.

We apologize for any inconvenience this delay may cause.

Sincerely,

Customer Service

Enclosure

FOLLOW-UP LETTER TO VERIFY THAT AN ADJUSTMENT WAS MADE

Making credit adjustments is a routine procedure that many companies handle with straightforward form letters like this one. The bracketed information would actually be filled in by hand on forms with blank spaces left for the appropriate entries.

Dear Cellular One Client,

This is to verify that the adjustment you requested was applied to your cellular account, #[acct. no.] on [adj. date]. The total amount of the adjustment is $[adj. amt.], and will appear on your next month's invoice.

The amount of the credit will either be subtracted from the total monthly activity next month (if you pay this month's bill in full) or it will appear both as a balance forward *and* a credit, which will cancel each other out (if you subtract the credit amount from this month's invoice).

In either case, the amount due will be correct.

If you need any further assistance, or have any other questions, please give us a call!

Sincerely,

Client Service Representative

RESPONDING TO COMPLAINT ABOUT BILLING ERROR

This letter combines a number of issues in one: a customer complaint, an apology for a company error, and confirmation of the customer's decision to cancel his subscription. The tone is friendly, cooperative, and understanding. The offer of a gift is intended to help mend the relationship and assure the customer that the newspaper cares.

May 5, 1995

Mr. Joseph Sweeney
33 W. Midway Drive, No. 664
Provo, UT 84094

Dear Mr. Sweeney,

Thank you for your letter of May 1. I agree that you should not have been billed for the two weeks of newspaper delivery you received. Consequently, I have asked our Accounting Department to credit your account for that amount.

I am sorry you have made the decision not to resubscribe to our paper. I can understand why you have reached that conclusion. If we can be of help to you in the future, please let me know. Please accept this umbrella as an apology for the problems you have had.

If I can be of further assistance to you in the future, please call me at 555-1102.

Sincerely yours,

J. Robert Stephens
Circulation Administration Manager

13 ■ MAKING REQUESTS OF CUSTOMERS

Occasionally, a company needs to request the help of its customers for one reason or another. The following letters provide examples of some of the situations that might generate a letter of request to a customer.

REQUESTING COOPERATION ON ORDER FULFILLMENT

This letter is primarily responding to customers who call in an order, then send a fax of the same order, then send a hard copy by mail. Consequently, the order department ends up with three orders for the same merchandise going to a single customer. After thanking the customer for the order, the letter explains the dilemma and the procedures for avoiding the problem in the future.

March 13, 1995

June Lovegren
Calapooya Computers Inc.
P.O. Box 1143
Kalamazoo, MI 48431

Dear Ms. Lovegren,

Thank you for your recent order with Symantec. Symantec receives a large number of orders via different methods, and this often leads to duplication of an order. These orders may be marked "Confirming Order," "Confirmation," "Confirming Copy," "Confirmation Only," "Confirmation of FAX," "Do Not Duplicate," or some other verbiage that suggests an order is already in house. Our Order Administration Department assumes that it should not process orders. Yet, when we search for the original order, it may be difficult to find because it was entered under a person's name or on our prepaid system.

In an effort to reduce the chances of duplicating your purchase order #1125-11, we ask that you verify that this purchase order is indeed the only copy we will receive, mark the copy with the words "This is an original purchase order and no other copy has or will be sent," and then please FAX it back to us at our toll-free fax number, 800-555-1102. If you do not have a FAX system available you may mail a copy of this letter attached to your purchase order with the above statement to 175 West Broadway, Eugene, OR 97401. Attn: Order Administration.

Thank you for your cooperation in this process. If you should have any questions, please contact Order Administration.

Sincerely,

Kate Webber
Order Administration Manager

REQUESTING RETURN OF DUPLICATE ORDER SHIPPED

The company made a mistake and sent two of the same product to a customer. When requesting that the customer return the duplicate order, the letter writer thanks her for the order, explains and apologizes for the error, and asks for the response. She does not go into the consequences of not returning the merchandise but operates on a level of trust that the customer will comply. If not—well, that's another letter!

July 16, 1995

Clara Queensfield
Sumatra Industries
9928 S.W. Fairfield Blvd.
Pittsburgh, PA 18312

Dear Ms. Queensfield,

Thank you for recent order. Unfortunately, we made an error during the processing of your request, which resulted in a duplicate shipment of the product you ordered.

We apologize for this error and any inconvenience it may have caused. Please call our Customer Service Department to allow us to arrange for the return of the over shipment. We will try to find the means most convenient to your schedule. I have enclosed both a Return Merchandise Authorization sticker for UPS pick-up and a postage-paid address label for return via U.S. Postal Service.

Again, our apologies for any inconvenience. I look forward to hearing from you.

Sincerely,

Lanette Miller
Customer Relations Department

REQUESTING CUSTOMER ASSISTANCE WITH SURVEY

Every once in a while it's a good idea to find out what your customers think about you. Are you on track with the products and services you offer? Are your customers generally satisfied? Are there problems out there that need to be addressed? A survey is a sophisticated tool, however, and it's important to get help from a professional in order to prepare a survey that will truly provide useful information. The letter below is the cover letter that accompanies the survey and asks for a small amount of the customer's time. Providing a gift with the survey often increases your rate of response.

March 16, 1995

Dear friend,

You have been a valued customer of Zenon Systems for some time now. We felt it was time that you were given a chance to tell us what you want in the future, what you like best about our current offerings, and what you would like to see changed.

Could you please take a moment to give us your thoughts?

We look forward to hearing your views. If you'd like to see the results of our survey, check the last box on the form and you'll receive a summary of customer responses. We'll also let you know our plans for responding to your input.

In appreciation for your help, we've enclosed a certificate for a free book from our technical support library, or 10 percent off your next order, whichever you prefer.

Thank you for your help.

Sincerely,

Paul Carruthers
Vice President, Customer Support

INVITING CUSTOMERS TO 100TH ANNIVERSARY OPEN HOUSE

When your company achieves important milestones, awards, or recognition or has impressive new products to introduce, invite your customers by for an open house. This is only feasible with companies catering to a local clientele, but the concept can apply to others. Chain operations can have simultaneous gatherings at locations across the country. Mail order companies can "invite" customers to toast the company's success with a gift certificate or coupon for a free bottle of champagne (or sparkling apple juice). Whatever the occasion, it's an opportunity to let your customers know you appreciate them. This letter is centered, like an invitation.

To our very special Oberon Manufacturing Customers:

We've got a good excuse to celebrate!
We hope you'll join us in toasting Oberon's 100th anniversary.

We know that, as our loyal customers, you are the reason
we've kept growing into a grand old age.
And your suggestions, comments—and complaints—
have kept us from getting stodgy or staid.

**Please drop by our open house
Friday, September 15
3 p.m. till the cows come home**

Help us celebrate a century of quality manufacturing!

For information, call Shari in Customer Service
555-1129

We look forward to seeing you!

MAINTAINING CUSTOMER RELATIONSHIP

What do you do when a good customer suddenly stops coming in? It's a good practice to keep in touch with your customers, asking for their honest feedback and assuring your commitment to providing the best possible service. When a customer suddenly stops coming in without explanation, you might want to send a letter like this one, asking if there was a problem and if there is any way to address it to the customer's satisfaction.

February 1, 1995

Lauren Dexter
Hillside Restaurant
3211 North Hillside Drive
Portland, ME 04110

Dear Lauren,

Thank you for using our laundry services for the past three years. We have enjoyed the opportunity to prepare your restaurant linens to your satisfaction. I am concerned, since you have not sent linens for the past week, that we may have in some way disappointed you. You are a valuable customer, and we don't want to lose your goodwill.

If something went wrong, please give us the opportunity to set it right and compensate for any problems. Our primary concern is always your complete satisfaction.

We look forward to hearing from you soon.

Sincerely,

Pamela Smith
Manager

TION

For further information or a current catalog, write:
NTC Business Books
a division of NTC Publishing Group
4255 West Touhy Avenue
Lincolnwood, Illinois 60646–1975 U.S.A.